James Jones
and the
Handy Writers'
Colony

James Jones

and the

Handy Writers' Colony

GEORGE HENDRICK, HELEN HOWE, AND DON SACKRIDER

Southern Illinois University Press
Carbondale and Edwardsville

Library of Congress Cataloging-in-Publication Data
Hendrick, George.
    James Jones and the Handy Writers' Colony / George Hendrick, Helen
    Howe, and Don Sackrider.
        p. cm.
    Includes bibliographical references and index.
        1. Jones, James, 1921–1977 — Homes and haunts — Illinois — Marshall.
    2. Artist colonies — Illinois — Marshall — History. 3. Authors, American —
    20th century — Biography. 4. Handy Writers' Colony — History. 5. Marshall
    (Ill.) — History. 6. Handy, Lowney Turner. 7. Handy, Harry. I. Howe,
Helen. II. Sackrider, Don. III. Title.

PS3560.O49 Z7 2001
813'.54 — dc21
[B]   00-032193
ISBN 0-8093-2365-6 (alk. paper)
ISBN 0-8093-2370-2 (pbk. : alk. paper)

The paper used in this publication meets the minimum requirements of
American National Standard for Information Sciences — Permanence of
Paper for Printed Library Materials, ANSI Z39.48-1992. ⊚

Contents

Illustrations

Acknowledgments

We are indebted to many people who helped us gather information for this study of Lowney and Harry Handy, James Jones, and the Handy Colony. Our research would have been impossible without our access to the Handy Colony Collection, which is housed in the Archives/Special Collections at the University of Illinois at Springfield. The archivist Thomas J. Wood and Professor Judith Everson, cocurators of the collection, have assisted us for many years, and they gave us permission to publish materials from the Handy collection (cited as UIS throughout this study). Wood and Meredith Keating prepared the excellent *James Jones in Illinois: A Guide to the Handy Writers' Colony Collection*, which has made our search for materials much easier. We have learned much from Wood's article "'Not Following in the Groove': Lowney Handy, James Jones, and the Handy Colony for Writers," in the *Illinois Historical Journal*.

When J. Michael Lennon and Jeffrey Van Davis were preparing their documentary, *James Jones: Reveille to Taps*, which aired on PBS in 1985 and 1986, they learned of the existence of the Handy collection, then in the possession of Margaret Turner, wife of the late Harold Turner, Lowney's brother. Margaret Turner donated the collection to Sangamon State University, now the University of Illinois at Springfield. We are especially indebted to Lennon and Davis for their work in bringing the Handy papers to their library and for making this large and important collection available to the scholarly community. We also had access to the Jones Collection at the University of Illinois at Urbana-Champaign. Our sincere thanks go to Barbara Jones, librarian of the Rare Book and Special Collection Library, where that collection is housed.

Members of the James Jones Literary Society have opened many avenues of research for us. This society was founded at Lincoln Trail College in Robinson, Illinois, and holds annual meetings. It publishes a newsletter and has instituted important literary awards. Past presidents of the society J. Michael Lennon, Judith Everson, and Jerry Bayne—as well as the current president, Ray Elliott—have been extremely helpful over a long period of time.

Dwight Connelly helped us acquire books by colonists. Alice Cornett provided us with biographical information about Lowney Handy. We are indebted to both of them. Tinks Howe and his mother were longtime friends of James Jones and of Lowney and Harry Handy. We want to thank Tinks for his contribution to this study. Jon Shirota gave us access to his intriguing play *The Last Retreat*, his letters from Lowney Handy, and his recollections of the colony. We greatly appreciate all of Jon's help.

As a way of recapturing the past, Helen and Tinks Howe and Don Sackrider wrote out their recollections of James Jones, Lowney and Harry Handy, and the colony. Jon Shirota also provided a narrative concerning his months at the colony and the influence Lowney had on him. We have drawn on these extensive narratives, sometimes paraphrasing them and at other times quoting directly from them. These narratives are in the personal possession of the authors.

Thomas J. Wood has granted us permission to use photographs from the Handy Colony Collection. He has also given us permission to quote from the papers of Charles Robb, including his poem "Khaki Moon," inspired by Jim Jones. J. Michael Lennon, editor of *Selected Poems of Charles Robb*, has also given his permission to quote from that work. In addition to those already named, we would like to acknowledge the help of Carl M. Becker, Steven R. Carter, Vanessa Faurie, James R. Giles, Juanita Martin, the late Charles Robb, and Robert G. Thobaben. Members of the James Jones Literary Society and panelists and speakers at the annual meetings have also provided valuable assistance.

James Jones
and the
Handy Writers'
Colony

Introduction:
Lowney, Harry, Jim, and the Colony

An unusual colony for writers in east-central Illinois, founded by Lowney and Harry Handy and James Jones, developed without institutional support and was the expression of the American pioneering spirit. Lowney (rhyming with *phony*)—the wife of Harry Handy, an oil company executive in Robinson, Illinois—was frustrated with middle-class life in small-town America. An unpublished writer interested in the writing craft, she had at first few contacts with agents or publishers or even other writers.[1] For a time she devoted herself to helping the down-and-out in Robinson, counseling them and giving them financial aid. Her life changed one day in 1943 when she met a deeply troubled soldier, James Jones, who wanted to be a writer. Lowney saw some of his work, believed he was a genius, and with her husband, Harry, took Jones into their home as soon as she could get him out of the army. She encouraged him, mothered him, loved him, and badgered him while he learned to write fiction. In the years that followed, Harry supported Jones financially even though he obviously knew that Lowney and Jim Jones were lovers.

Lowney taught Jim what she knew, went over his writing line by line, argued with him, cajoled him, praised his work. Jim was a psychologically wounded man in those years, and Lowney became his warden, controlling his life. The winters were harsh in Robinson, and she began taking Jim to quiet Florida beach towns in the winter. When Jim had written a considerable part of a promising manuscript, *From Here to Eternity*, Lowney began to seek out other young men interested in writing, whom she took on as students. Even before Jim's first novel was published, Lowney had been dreaming of a permanent colony, and she and Harry and Jim began to build a summer camp in a meadow owned by Harry's mother in nearby Marshall, Illinois. Harry paid the bills and oversaw the construction of some of the houses and barracks at the colony. Jim's novel was a success, and other students came to study with his mentor. They all became part of an unusual, even quirky, creative writing colony.

Today, creative writing programs at the undergraduate and graduate levels are found throughout the United States, and since the end of World War II, the number of universities offering a master of fine arts degree in creative writing has expanded tremendously. Almost all these programs use the workshop method—where students work in a seminar setting, reading and commenting on each other's works and conferring with the professor who conducts the workshop. The students are expected to read widely, to avail themselves of the cultural events and intellectual life of the campus. In addition there are a few colonies such as Yaddo and MacDowell that provide room and board and privacy for writers, who meet for a social hour after dinner each day. Writing programs and writing colonies are built on virtually the same principles throughout the country.

The Handy Colony, chartered by the state of Illinois in 1951 but operating informally from 1943, was different. It reflected the unique philosophy and forceful personality of Lowney Handy, who believed she could teach anyone to write. The Handy Colony was experimental—over the years Lowney had developed her own unusual methodology. Before they could begin their own novels, her students spent a considerable time copying word for word texts by major writers such as Hemingway or Faulkner or Fitzgerald. Instead of encouraging her students to read widely, Lowney had her list of approved and disapproved texts. Instead of having students critique each other's work, she alone read each student's work-in-progress. Students were not allowed to talk to each other about their work-in-progress. She believed (as did Jim) that anything talked about was lost, talked out, and that writers and artists became dilettantes if they discussed their work. Her students, completely subsidized, lived in Spartan accommodations, and she controlled their lives. They copied or did their own writing in the mornings and worked at various odd jobs and played sports on the colony grounds during the afternoons. She preferred to work with male renegades and castaways who had seen some of the worst of what the world had to offer, but she also taught several women, who generally had also experienced difficult lives. She warned her male students to avoid marital entanglements; she felt they could satisfy their sexual urges with whores.

Lowney could charm anyone with her honeyed voice, making them feel special and unique. She was a nonconformist, a Democrat in a Republican rural area, a freethinker in a conservative community. No longer interested in the country club set, she was a transcendentalist drawing wisdom from Hindu and theosophical texts. She rejected middle-class materialistic values. She was an avid, self-taught reader, very charismatic, but also dominating and opinionated. Her language was every bit as salty as that of the veterans returning from World War II. She and her husband were childless; they had an open marriage. She was a failed writer, but she developed into a shrewd editor of fiction. She had lived most of her life in small towns in east-central Illinois.

Harry, a 1923 graduate in engineering from the University of Illinois, became superintendent of the Ohio Oil Company refinery in 1947. He was shrewd in business, was trained to oversee construction, and was certainly useful when the colony was being built, diverting men and equipment from the refinery to that project. He was financially successful and willingly supported the colony and its students. He never wavered in his support of Lowney and her wishes and desires. He was also judicious and had the ability to calm emotional scenes. Without Harry, Lowney would have found it difficult to establish and maintain the Handy Colony.

How did Lowney, Harry, and Jim come to found a colony? How did she get students? Some of the answers to these questions can be found in A. B. C. Whipple's article "James Jones and His Angel: His Talent Lay Buried Under Frustration and Rebellion Until an Illinois Housewife Made Him Write 'From Here to Eternity,'" which appeared in *Life* magazine on May 7, 1951. According to Whipple, when Jim and Lowney met for the first time in November 1943, it was the "biggest day" in Jim's life (142). He was then a down-and-out soldier not long out of hospitals, gone AWOL. He returned to his hometown of Robinson, Illinois, where he went on a long drunk. His aunt Sadie then looked to Lowney Handy for help.

Lowney was described by Whipple as a housewife, married to an engineer at the Ohio Oil Company. The photograph of the Handys showed Harry to be a distinguished-looking man, aristocratic in bearing; she was dressed casually and was smiling broadly. They appeared to be happily married. The story does indicate that Lowney was rebellious and that her concern for Robinson's drunks, delinquents, and pregnant unmarried girls brought her into conflict with the Handys' social set.

Jim's troubled history is recounted in the story: his unhappy childhood, the lack of money that forced him to join the army instead of attending college, his army life in Hawaii, his being injured on Guadalcanal, the death of his mother and the suicide of his father while he was in the service. "By the time he reached the hospital at Camp Campbell, Kentucky," Whipple wrote, "he was a whimpering neurotic. It was like a case of shellshock, complicated by all the long list of disappointments he had had since his earliest childhood" (144).

The article then turns to the meeting of Jim and Lowney and her unerring instinct that he was a genius, a writer of great potential. Lowney told the story of her getting Jim out of the army and (a sanitized account) of taking him into her home, building a room for him, supporting him as he learned to write, acting as overseer to keep him at work. The Whipple story is almost a fairy tale: A rebellious young man wrote *From Here to Eternity*, one of the sensational successes of twentieth-century literature, under the stern sponsorship and guidance of an Illinois housewife. Like most fairy tales, this one is romanticized, as we will show in the first three chapters.

Jones's *From Here to Eternity* was a publishing sensation when it appeared in the late winter of 1950–1951. Sales were enormous, film rights were quickly sold, and reviews of the gritty novel were mostly laudatory. Perhaps the romantic and financial aspects of the story are what made Whipple's article such a defining piece of journalism. There were large numbers of Americans who wanted to be writers, and most envisioned that writing would make them rich. The *Life* article mythologized Lowney Handy, her first student, and the school for writing itself, making it clear that Lowney had something valuable to offer would-be writers. She had gathered around her the Handy Artists Group (later to be called the Handy Colony).

Before *Eternity* was completed, according to Whipple, she realized that she had time to take on other problem cases, and began to take in other aspiring writers. In the summer she took them to a farm pasture in Marshall, Illinois, and in the winter to Florida. She was already receiving letters from young people wanting to join the group, and the Whipple article brought in many more:

> When she thinks she has really found someone she asks him to come and see her. If he looks as if he will fit into the Group, he is given a trial. It is not an easy trial. For at least two months . . . he gets what Lowney calls the Treatment. He does the dirty work. . . . Meanwhile he is permitted to write nothing on his own. Depending on the line Lowney thinks his talent is taking, she makes a selection of books and sets him to work on them. He does not just read them; he copies them, word for word, all the way through. He does this for at least a month, sometimes two. Then he starts writing and getting brutal criticism from the rest of the Group. Most of the would-be writers give up under the Treatment. . . . Those who remain, and those Lowney does not kick out, become full-fledged members of the Group. (153)

The outlines of Whipple's account are correct, but the "brutal criticism" came from Lowney, not from "the Group."

Many of the would-be writers had already survived boot camp. Why not go through torture and let Lowney guide them to success? All the colonists knew she had good contacts in the publishing world. She worked in other ways to sell or publicize books by colonists as well. Before *Eternity* was published, she would go into a bookstore, buy fifty books, and tell the owner of the store and the clerks about Jones's forthcoming novel. She would introduce him; show copies of letters he had received from America's best-known editor, Maxwell Perkins; she would assure everyone in hearing distance that Jim would soon join the ranks of Perkins's successes like Wolfe, Fitzgerald, and Hemingway. She would send follow-up letters to the bookstores about the progress of the novel. Wherever she went with Jim, she worked at selling *Eternity*. On a smaller scale she worked at selling the books of later colonists; she talked about their works in bookstores and gave interviews.

Harry had been giving Lowney four hundred dollars a month to support her school—a considerable sum in those days. Jim was putting much of his royalty money into the colony, which expanded and grew in reputation from 1951 to 1957. Then Jim broke with Lowney after a sensational episode following his marriage to the beautiful, talented Gloria Mosolino. The colony survived for several more years, and Lowney did develop several talented writers; about seventy students came to the colony for long or short stays, and ten of them published novels and stories.

The following story recounts the complex relationships among Lowney, Harry, Jim, and the Handy colonists. Some of the colonists rebelled against Lowney and her ways, but most of them felt her influence on them was profound. She, Jones, and the colony itself all came to take on mythic qualities. The Handy Colony has been both extravagantly praised and fiercely derided. It is the intention here to tell—both dispassionately and sympathetically—the story of the three founders of the colony and of the writers who came there to work.

1
Lowney Turner Handy:
The Early Life of a "Literary Angel"

W hat was left unsaid in the *Life* article turns out to be much more intriguing than what Lowney, Jim, Harry, and A. B. C. Whipple, the nominal author of the piece, were willing to publish. In the article, for instance, little is explained about Lowney's past and how she came to be a literary angel. Lowney Turner was born on April 15 or 16, 1904 (accounts vary, but she celebrated the sixteenth), in the Bluegrass region of Kentucky, in White Hall, the mansion of an eccentric called Cassius Marcellus Clay. Her father was a worker on the Clay estate. How she came to be born in the mansion and named for Clay's son is a remarkable story, which became a part of the Turner family mythology and was to influence Lowney's later life.

Lowney's father, James Turner (1880–1959), was born in a cabin with a dirt floor on Red Lick Mountain, near Berea, Kentucky. This was a region where men were armed and bloody feuds were commonplace. Lowney often claimed that her grandfather Turner had killed three men and that her father's youngest brother, Willie, one day argued with his wife over a dog, then killed her and the dog, thus starting a mountain feud. Willie was himself killed in a churchyard within a few weeks.

Jim Turner was one of seven children, and his father died when he was nine. He had about three years of schooling and, after the death of his father, went to work in Richmond, Kentucky, as a kitchen helper and errand boy. By the time he was in his teens he was a groom on Cassius Marcellus Clay's estate, located between Lexington and Richmond. He possessed both a speaking voice and a personality inherited by Lowney. He met Fanny Carpenter (1882–1957), daughter of a financially successful timber buyer for a railroad, when she was a student at the Madison Female Academy. Clay encouraged Jim Turner's romantic interest in the young woman, even though her social standing was much higher than that of the handsome hillbilly groom in the stables.

Fanny's mother, Mrs. Quiller Carpenter, a very authoritarian woman, was opposed to her daughter's interest in the uneducated mountaineer. Mrs. Carpenter, herself part Cherokee, was a woman of severe looks and disposition (as head-strong as her granddaughter Lowney was to be). Unlike her husband, she was not even tempered. As the romance between the two young people flourished, Mrs. Carpenter remarked: "Fanny has driven her geese to a poor market. . . . Hope they aren't planning on getting married. Just more babies to take care of." She praised Jim as coming "a long way in spite of his lack of education" (McClellan 17–18).[1] Fanny was as strong-willed as her mother and insisted on marrying Jim Turner.

Jim Turner and Fanny Carpenter were married on Christmas Day, 1901, in the living room of the Carpenter home. Fanny had been provided with an extensive trousseau. The young couple lived in a four-room house on the Clay estate for the next few years. Jim Turner was a handsome, intelligent man with an outgoing personality, and a honeyed speaking voice (inherited by Lowney). He was on good terms with his employer, the Lion of White Hall. Fanny Turner was well educated for that time, more refined than her mountaineer husband, proud of her Kentucky heritage. Her mother had been correct: there were many babies to take care of—twelve were born and nine survived infancy (McClellan 1–19).

Cassius Marcellus (Cash) Clay (1810–1903), cousin of Henry Clay, was born in the older section of the White Hall mansion. Educated in Kentucky and at Yale, he became an abolitionist, which brought him into conflict with the citizens of his home state. He was to become a Republican in a region where Democrats were an absolute majority. Except for mountaineers, who typically were not slaveholders, many Kentucky voters were strong supporters of the peculiar institution. "That old son of a bitch" was a typical description of Cash Clay. "He went against his time, against his own people" (Richardson xi–xii).

A handsome, independent, cultured man, Cash Clay was also moody and dangerous, a fighter notorious for his dueling who faced his enemies with knives, guns, and cannons. His most courageous act in antebellum Kentucky was to found a newspaper in Lexington in 1845—the *True American*, "devoted to gradual and constitutional emancipation." The paper was met with hostility, and Clay, suspecting the possibility of mob action, fortified the newspaper office with two brass cannons. If the mob did make it into the building, Clay planned to detonate a keg of powder and send as many of the mob as possible "into eternity" (Richardson 43–46).

At a time when agitation was growing against the *True American*, Clay became seriously ill with typhoid fever. He knew well "that slavery and a free press could not live together." Indeed, the slavery forces triumphed during Clay's extended illness, and a group illegally packed up the press and shipped it to Cincinnati, where the paper was published for a time. After recovering from his illness, Clay wrote that "the Constitutional liberties of Kentucky [were] overthrown; and an irresponsible despotism of slave-holding established in their ruins" (Richardson 54).

After the election of 1860, Lincoln appointed Cash Clay minister to Russia, where (always heavily armed with bowie knives) he moved easily among the royalty, the aristocracy, and the peasants. His wife returned to Kentucky during his Russian years, and after her departure, he apparently had an affair with a ballerina, perhaps the mysterious Annie Petroff. Clay acquired a painting of a beautiful dancer and later placed it in his Kentucky mansion. It was believed that the ballerina was the mother of his son.

When Cash returned to Kentucky, his marriage went through troubled times, though his wife remained mistress of White Hall. One night during a gala at the mansion, with many social figures from the Bluegrass in the elegant ballroom, one or two heavily veiled women (the number varies in the accounts) arrived by carriage at the front door.

"General Clay," a woman said, "I have brought you your son from Russia."

Clay bowed and asked, "May I take him up into the light and look at him?"

Satisfied with what he saw, Clay then introduced Leonide Petroff, who was to be renamed Launey Clay, as "my adopted son from Russia" (Richardson 118).

Launey's arrival caused an uproar at White Hall, for the boy was assumed to be Clay's son. Mrs. Clay soon left the estate and moved to Lexington, where she sued for divorce. Many conservatives in the Bluegrass state were outraged. Clay was not one to be moved by public opinion, however. He remarked, "Some women of Richmond of doubtful reputation tried to drive Launey and myself from society." His own daughters were highly critical of him. An editor of the *Cincinnati Enquirer* fulminated, "You see an early champion of freedom walking about boastfully with a bastard son, imported like an Arabian cross-horse, and swearing at his family" (Richardson 118).

Stories circulated about Launey's mother. Was she the ballerina in the portrait? A member of the aristocracy? Was the boy really Clay's illegitimate son? Or did he adopt the child from the Petroffs? Clay let the stories multiply and enjoyed the notoriety. Jim and Fanny Turner obviously knew the stories and the rumors about the beautiful woman in the portrait and the alleged love child, but it was only Jim who would talk about the "scandal." Fanny Turner was a proper Baptist woman who would ignore the sordid escapades of Cash Clay.

After Launey grew up and moved away from White Hall, Clay was a lonely old man. Wealthy and eccentric, he decided in 1894 to remarry. He had become attracted to Dora McClelland, then about fifteen. His family tried to prevent the union but Clay outwitted them, and the ceremony was performed.

By this time Clay, ever fearful of enemies, had fortified the mansion with guns and the brass cannons he had brought to his newspaper office years before. A reporter who interviewed Clay at the time of his second marriage wrote, "Some think the old General is crazy, but I do not think so." The reporter did think he might be in his "second childhood," but "his mind is as clear as a bell" (Richardson 129). Many local citizens felt that Clay in taking a young bride was a menace to public morality, and the sheriff and a small contingent of men rode out to White Hall to rescue Dora. Clay kept the cannons loaded. The results were predictable. Cash drove the posse away.

Clay lived with his bride for a time, but after two years she left, divorced him, and remarried. Clay, alone again, became even more peculiar. Clay's family went to court to have the old man declared incompetent, but Jim Turner argued that his boss was childish, not insane. Jim knew the old man well, for he often drove him around the estate and was regarded as a trusted employee. His loyalty to the Lion of White Hall was to gain him the enmity of some of Clay's children (McClellan 26).

After Cash's death on July 22, 1903, the mansion needed to be protected while the estate was being settled. An auction of Cash Clay's personal items was held on October 8, 1903, and the oil portrait of the ballerina was sold. A respected young worker, by this time an overseer on the estate, Jim Turner was asked to move into White Hall with his wife, and they did. They had by this time already lost two babies and were expecting their third. One day Fanny Turner was working in the formal rose garden and uncovered a spoon in the dirt. It was, as Lowney's sister remembered, "delicately carved, and stamped in the bowl was the name 'Lowney'" (the Turners must have misread the script). Mrs. Turner was superstitious (as her daughter Lowney was later to be) and considered it an omen. The Turners decided to name their next baby "Lowney," whether it was a boy or a girl. The baby was a girl, and she was called Lowney (McClellan 20–22).

Vivian Turner McClellan wrote in her autobiography, *One in the Middle*, that her sister Lowney "had curly black hair, piercing brown eyes, and was a little spitfire. Maybe Lowney drew some of her spunk from the owner of the house where she was born" (23). We can also speculate that the mythology surrounding the painting of the ballerina hanging in White Hall was partially responsible for Lowney's later interest in ballet and in the arts in general. The life of the violent, unconventional Cash Clay was often discussed within the

Turner family circle, and the stories greatly influenced Lowney. She was to be as unconcerned about public opinion as he was.

The Turners went on living in White Hall after Lowney was born. The guns and cannons were still in place, and when the child was a toddler Fanny complained, "Jim, do we have to keep all these guns in here?" She also remarked, "Scares me to death to see Lowney climbing all over those cannons. Going to bust her head wide open one of these days!" (23)

Fanny Turner did not like living in the mansion, especially when her husband was away. Many of the personal items and furnishings had been sold and the huge mansion was undoubtedly gloomy. Lowney was proving an imaginative child. Fanny complained to her husband, "Lowney won't get out of my sight. Don't know what has gotten into her. Keeps talking about seeing a ghost in the little bedroom upstairs." Jim thought his daughter had been listening to too many stories told by the "little Negro children" on the estate (23–24).

Fanny Turner's dissatisfactions grew strong enough to cause them to move into a small house near the stables. Their daughter Sue was born there. Jim Turner decided to look for another job; he had previously been in conflict with Clay's children from Clay's first marriage when they were having their father declared incompetent, and he perhaps felt his position on the estate was not secure. At any rate, it happened one time he rode up to Illinois on a horse from the stables. Upon his return he was charged with horse theft. Although he was eventually exonerated, the case against her husband with all its turmoil was particularly difficult for the conventional Fanny Turner. Her emotional problems were compounded by illness (she survived a ruptured appendix, and she later suffered from severe neuritis). She was confined to bed for months, her daughter Vivian wrote, and "The illness left her in a highly nervous condition from which she never fully recovered" (26). Lowney, like her mother, had periods of nervousness and agitation.

Fanny Turner and the children lived with her parents during her illnesses. One family story from this time is particularly revealing: Lowney was jealous of Sue, for she did not like being out of the limelight. Once her grandmother Carpenter found Lowney on top of the sewing machine about to drop the baby to the floor. Lowney said, "I don't like this baby. We don't need her around here" (25–27). The anecdote reflects sibling rivalry, but it also foreshadows Lowney's reaction to Jones's bride, Gloria. Lowney did not want to lose Jones, she disliked the beautiful Gloria, and she came to feel that Gloria should be gotten rid of.

Lowney Turner's parents were poor, but she was born in a mansion. The great man of the neighborhood was Cash Clay, an eccentric, violent, independent character who cared not a whit for public opinion. She was named for a love child, and later when she was influenced by theosophy and several Oriental religions she claimed that in a previous life she had been a

Russian ballerina. She was always, from early childhood, imaginative, independent, willful, as intent on having her own way as Cash Clay was in having his. The life and legends of Clay became part of her emotional life. She had violence in her blood from the Turner family and from the legends about Clay. This was of particular importance when she was helping James Jones with *From Here to Eternity*, especially in the scenes concerning Prewitt's childhood in Kentucky. She was as emotional as Cash Clay and as her mother, but through yoga she attempted to control these conflicting passions. She remained, however, a demanding, authoritarian personality, certainly a well-known type in the Kentucky of her parents' early lives and her own childhood at White Hall. She also inherited the good looks of her mother and father and their native intelligence. From her father whom she adored she inherited an outgoing personality and his sweet honeyed voice.

Jim Turner, after being cleared of the horse-theft charges, returned to Illinois and found a job on a farm with relatives who lived near Charleston. In 1909 or 1910, he sent for his wife and children who had remained with her parents in Kentucky. These were difficult years for the growing family. Jim moved from one job to another, from farm work to construction work on an interurban streetcar line. They were especially difficult years for Fanny, accustomed as she was to the support of her parents and cousins during the time of her extended illness. In Illinois, since they were poor, she did all the housework and tended to the children.

Finally, Jim found employment as a section hand on the Pennsylvania Railroad and the family moved to the village of Dennison, near Marshall, Illinois. The family lived in a converted store building that had a large room and a small room on the first floor and a large room on the second floor, reached by an outside stairway. It was an awkward arrangement, and remodeling was eventually carried out, carving out proper rooms and an indoor stairs. Still, the building always looked like a store, and the Turners were made to feel that they lived on the wrong side of the tracks (McClellan 29–30).

By the time Lowney and her younger sister Sue were in the third and second grades respectively, their need for school clothes was great, but there was no money, so Fanny decided to turn the elaborate dresses from her trousseau into school dresses for the little girls. The result was not what the Turners expected. The other children in Dennison, perhaps out of envy, jeered at Lowney and Sue: "You kids don't talk like we do, kinda hillbilly." Others chimed in, "Yeah, Kentucky hillbillies." Sue was placid by nature, but Lowney was "quick tempered and as mean as the dickens" (31). Lowney pummelled her tormentors, and after a few skirmishes the taunting stopped. In one account (which may have been fictionalized), Lowney wrote that she took special revenge on Anna, one of her tormentors. A day after one skirmish, Lowney had an idea and formed a plan. In the country school Anna sat directly behind her: "I adjusted my position for an accurate throw (this came automatically as I was then pitching on the boys baseball team), loosened the cork in a large bottle of black ink and slung the contents over my left shoulder. I then began to gasp and stood up in my seat calling the attention of the entire school to myself as I had spilt part of the ink on my left arm. 'Oh, the stopper flew out,' were my astounded words" (manuscript, UIS). Lowney was hardly an ordinary, proper, Victorian girl.

Inevitably, Lowney was to clash with her mother's pious Victorian views. Fanny Turner was a member of the Missionary Baptist Church and intent upon instilling in her children traditional Christian beliefs. Lowney was seldom traditional; she was independent and outspoken. She greeted a visiting preacher, "Come in if your nose is clean" (28). As an adult Lowney espoused nontraditional religious views far from those of her mother, liberally mixing theosophical and Hindu beliefs with Christianity.

As the oldest child, Lowney was the authoritarian organizer whenever she was away from her mother's watchful eyes. She learned to use her storytelling skills. One night when she and Sue had four girlfriends sleeping over, their baby sister Gladys was a tag-along and crawled in bed with Lowney and Sue. As a way of getting rid of Gladys, Lowney told a story about the ghost she had seen at White Hall. McClellan's re-creation of the scene indicates Lowney's talents and the sometimes unexpected results: "Her spooky rendition was exciting and breathtaking and made their flesh creep and crawl. Gladys sat on the edge of the bed with open mouth and hanging breathlessly on every word. When Lowney got to the scary part, she let out an ungodly shriek, grabbing Gladys. Gladys went flabby and slumped off the bed onto the floor." Gladys had to be revived with cold water in her face, and Mrs. Turner's temper rose: "You kids nearly scared that 'youngun' to death. I ought to wear you all out. Don't let me ever hear of you doing a trick like that again" (37–38).

Fanny Carpenter also used folk and herbal remedies. When Gladys was seriously ill with mumps, measles, and whooping cough all at the same time, the medicines from the local doctor did not seem to help, and Mrs. Turner turned to folk remedies that had come to her from her Native American and European ancestors. Much later, when traditional medicine had a stronger hold in American society, Lowney, perhaps influenced by her mother's acceptance of folk remedies, was quite willing to use remedies such as fasting and enemas. She disliked taking doctor-prescribed medicines.

Her father, Jim Turner, was capable and well liked and was promoted from section hand to railroad detective. He was more interested in farming and in buying and selling horses and cattle, however, and he moved his family to a farm he was buying five miles from Marshall. Life was more difficult on the farm, for there was little income, and sudden disasters such as the death of most of their cattle kept the family poor.

Although the family lived in poverty, Fanny Turner, proud of her Bluegrass Kentucky heritage and her attendance at an academy, wanted her children to have a good education. When they were old enough, Lowney and Sue entered Marshall High School, driving a buggy or a cart (if the roads were particularly muddy) the five miles to school. Lowney was bright and independent. In his article, Whipple says that Lowney was "the only girl on the high school baseball team—and the pitcher at that. She became the school rebel. She ignored most of the girls, met the boys on their own level, . . . and gave not a damn for the talk it caused" (142). Lowney seems to have been mythologizing when she told Whipple she was a pitcher on the boys' baseball team at Marshall High School; her high school annual indicates she was a member of the girls basketball team. She did pitch on the baseball team of the country school she attended before entering Marshall High School. She was apparently the despair of her teachers. The 1922–1923 high school annual for her senior year notes: "She wiggles in the assembly / And drives the teachers wild."

At Marshall High School, the sisters were again ridiculed. Few country children went to high school, and Lowney and Sue heard comments such as "Why don't those country kids stay out on the farm where they belong?" When one Marshall boy learned Lowney was planning to try out for the Debating Club, he said, "We don't want that country hick on our team." Lowney joined the team and they won all their debates (McClellan 91–92).

Lowney took pleasure in playing pranks, letting a mouse loose in study hall, in calling attention to herself. At the same time, she had a secret life in literature; her sister Vivian wrote that Lowney was a lover of poetry and would read aloud to Vivian from her favorites such as "The Highwayman" by Alfred Noyes, "Annabel Lee" and "The Raven" by Edgar Allan Poe, and "The Congo" by Vachel Lindsay (95).

Jim Turner started a charge account at a Marshall drugstore to allow his daughters to purchase school supplies. Lowney and Sue also bought a compact, lipstick, and eyebrow pencils. Lowney was obviously the ringleader in this attempt to be as well made-up as the city girls (92–95).

Within the confines of the family farm, however, Lowney could not wear makeup, and she was carefully protected from boys. The arrival of the mail carrier was a big event in the lives of the Turner children, for he was often their only contact with the outside world. One summer the regular carrier was on vacation and the substitute was Harry Handy, son of a wealthy Marshall judge and a student in engineering at the University of Illinois. The elder Turners had heard that Harry was "fast" and "sowing a few wild oats." Mrs. Turner would not let any of the children go near the mailbox while he was in sight, but Lowney would usually disappear from the house and climb to the top of a maple tree or go to the barn loft to watch the reportedly "fast" Harry in his late-model sport car deliver the mail (130–31). Still in high school, Lowney wanted a way out of her poverty-stricken life, out of the religious and social convictions of her parents (especially those of her mother, but also of her overprotective father) and away from the constant squabbling of her younger brothers and sisters. The Turners were a contentious lot and not always congenial with each other. They were also clannish, however, and when one Turner was under attack they all stood together against the world. Marriage to Harry Handy was one way out for Lowney. This was the route she was eventually to take.

Jim Turner had always been an outgoing man, making friends everywhere. He was elected road commissioner in his precinct, and leaders of the Democratic party asked him in 1922 to stand for election as sheriff of Clark County. He bought an old Model T Ford and spent weeks electioneering. He became friendly with Mr. Calvin, a Jewish merchant in Marshall who began to purchase unsalted butter from the Turners. Through this merchant's relatives and friends in Terre Haute, the Turners began to sell more produce, bringing in much-needed money. Jim Turner, from a mountain family, was not prejudiced against African Americans or Jews. Turner was not a churchgoer as his wife was, and this may have protected him from adopting some racial and religious prejudices. He was a superb politician, and this also may have played a part in his acceptance of blacks and Jews. He needed their votes. His wife was prejudiced against Catholics but tempered her anti-Catholicism somewhat after one of her sons married a Catholic. Lowney, like her father, did not until late in her life express the usual racial and religious prejudices that were common in east-central Illinois, and even when she did express prejudiced views, it was most often in times of emotional turmoil when she was not her usual self.

The Republican candidate, a Mr. Barker, was wealthy. He was certain that he would easily defeat Jim Turner. On election evening he and his friends gathered at the sheriff's office in the courthouse to await word of victory. Turner went to the barbershop owned by Squab Wilson, an African American, to meet with his friends to await news. At midnight he was announced the winner of the election. Barker's reaction was, "I can't believe that Jim Turner has beaten me. How could he have? He's just a Kentucky hillbilly and horse trader. Well, if that don't beat all. Why that Jim Turner doesn't even own a decent suit of clothes" (McClellan 144).

Mr. Calvin passed on the comments about Jim not having a good suit to relatives in Terre Haute, and a Jewish merchant there outfitted him with two suits of clothes. Then the merchant added, "We want you to bring your wife over, so she can pick out things for herself and the children." Jim Turner's "friendship with Mr. Calvin and others hasn't gone unnoticed," the Terre Haute merchant remarked (144–45). In the 1920s when the KKK with its anti-Negro, anti-Jewish hatred was strong in the Midwest, Jim Turner was a politician who did not share the religious and racial hatreds of many in his time and place.

The Turners moved from the farm to living quarters at the county jail. Fanny Turner provided the food for the prisoners. The bemused reaction of many townspeople—as their meager belongings were moved into the jail— was to say: "That must be the new sheriff and his family. I heard he had a string of kids. Wife's kinda pretty, isn' she? I'd hate to take care of all those kids, but I guess you could lock them up" (148). The Turners did fit into life in the small Illinois town. The children all went to the local schools, and their years of great economic hardship were over. Jim Turner was gregarious and busy with his new duties. His wife stayed at home; her family and her church took all her time.

As much as possible, Lowney continued her independent ways. She could, with parental permission, entertain boyfriends on the front porch, but she and Sue were not allowed to date. Lowney knew about sneaking out at night, however, and asked Sue to double date with her and her boyfriend. Sue's date was special, Lowney told her: "He's a light-weight prize fighter and has a boxing match in Terre Haute tonight. He'll get us free passes if you'll be his date." Lowney and Sue announced that night they were going to their room to study for exams the next day, put dummies in their bed, and climbed out the window to meet the boys. Mrs. Turner discovered they were missing and waited for her daughters to return. Sue's date had been in a brutal fight, and Sue had vomited on her mother's coat, which she had borrowed without permission. When Lowney and Sue returned, their mother's anger was alleviated by Sue's condition. She told them, "I want you both to know that Sue being sick has saved you from being skinned alive. I don't think it's fair to punish one and not the other" (192–94).

Lowney continued her rebellious ways. She told Don Sackrider in December 1947 that, at the age of eighteen, she had slept with a young man because she did not know anything about sex and felt dumb and unsophisticated. Lowney apparently told others that Harry was the father of her unborn child, that he paid for the abortion, and since he felt guilty she forced him to marry her. The truth cannot be uncovered now, and it may well be that all these accounts are untrue or exaggerated. Whatever the facts, it is clear that Lowney was a nonconformist.

Lowney wanted to escape her mother's authoritarian ways. As soon as she finished high school in 1923 she left Marshall to work as a clerk in Georgetown, Illinois. The next year Sue finished high school, and the two went to Indianapolis to work. Lowney was always able to find a job; but she would have trouble keeping it. She did not like to get up early, and she certainly did not like to take orders. One of her bosses said of her, "That Lowney Turner isn't worth the powder it takes to paint her face" (195–96). Lowney seldom returned to Marshall, though she did spend one summer at home taking a business course at the high school.

Lowney found a way out of her unsuccessful life in Indianapolis by marrying Harry Handy in the summer of 1926. According to Alice Cornett, Harry spent the summer in Whiting, Indiana, at the Ohio Oil refinery, preparing drawings for construction at the Robinson refinery where he worked. On July 31 Harry and Lowney went to the courthouse at Crown Point, Indiana, and took out a marriage license. They were married later that day by a Justice of the Peace. No members of his or her family were present.

The account of their early married life she gave to Whipple for the *Life* article was true in its general outlines. Harry was indeed an engineer at the refinery in Robinson, twenty-eight miles south of Marshall. (His entire professional life was spent working for the Ohio Oil Company.) The couple lived in a rented house. "Lowney interested herself in bridge and sewing, cooked Harry's meals and got ready to raise a big family. But the children did not come" (143). What was left unsaid in the article was that Harry, an inveterate womanizer, infected Lowney with gonorrhea, and she had to have a hysterectomy. From that time on, it appears that Lowney and Harry had no sexual life together. They slept in separate bedrooms and led separate lives. Harry was a heavy drinker and continued to find female companionship away from home. Lowney hinted to Don Sackrider that she had had a few minor affairs. Lowney often told the story of her infection and its results and Jones used a fictionalized version of it in depicting the marriage of Captain Holmes and his wife, Karen, in the novel From Here to Eternity.

Lowney fought to save her marriage. Don Sackrider's mother told him that she was acquainted with one of Harry's girlfriends, a slim woman short enough to make Harry feel tall. The girl told Don's mother that Lowney had offered her a lot of money to quit seeing Harry. Don's mother was surprised by Lowney's actions, but Don believed that Lowney must have felt the affair had gone on long enough to threaten her marriage to Harry. After Harry died and Lowney was living with Don, she remarked one time that Harry had been the brick wall she leaned on, that he was the stable one and she was all show out in front.

The Handys' marriage was never broken; from their many surviving letters it is clear they stayed together because of love and affection. Lowney was intent on helping Harry get ahead, and she knew how to play the role of a devoted wife. The couple were part of the country club circle, and Lowney, using the Bluegrass training she had received from her mother, knew how to dress and act the part of the wife of an executive. The Handys bought a house, and Lowney filled it with antiques. She was a gourmet cook and a charming, vivacious hostess. The politics of Harry's appointment as superintendent of the refinery was complicated, and over many years Lowney played the political games with superb aplomb. As Whipple tells it, she said, "'But I was about to die yawning, . . .' She thought back to 'my years in the jail' and to the people with the absorbing problems she had known then. She began to search for people like that in Robinson. Soon she was visiting and occasionally giving some small financial help to the town's juvenile delinquents, the alcoholics, the unmarried mothers" (143). Indeed, Lowney's departure from the conventional life of upper-middle class women in mid-century, mid-continental America caused much talk in Robinson, especially after she began to help young servicemen and to invite bright high school students into her home. In Robinson, where there was little cultural or intellectual life, she began buying and reading large numbers of books. She discussed these books with the students and loaned them her books.

Lowney did not mention to Whipple in any detail that, in the 1930s, she had become interested in writing and had enrolled in at least one correspondence course. On June 23, 1936, she submitted a paper, "Write Me as One Who Loves His Fellow-Men." Poorly written though it is, it shows one of Lowney's preoccupations: her Native American heritage. She wrote that she was only "one thirty-second Indian" but, although the amount was small, "it has had the greatest influence on my life." She made it clear how that Indian blood had affected her: "I must be stoic and brave, loyal or revengeful to friend or foe." She would as a child hold lighted matches to her arms and smell the "scorching flesh" to show that she could suffer in silence. In a revision of this essay, she wrote, "I have never had a sense of fear; but, to this day I have not been able to assume that stoic calm of my worshipped forbears" (manuscript, UIS). It was the search for a stoic calm that led Lowney to another of her enthusiasms, theosophy. She read, admired, and annotated the works of Madame Blavatsky, Annie Besant, and many others interested in the occult. As a way of controlling her body and her emotions, she practiced yoga.

As Lowney moved away from small-town midwestern conventions, she turned increasingly to her new religious beliefs and to her writing. She did not accept the advice of her correspondence course teacher about her own writing, however (though later she did not hesitate to give strongly worded advice to her students at the colony). The essay she submitted to a University of Illinois extension class on June 23, 1936, was out of focus and undisciplined. She received a generous C plus. Lowney was later to say that such courses were useless. Apparently unfazed by early criticism of her writing, she began to draw up outlines for three novels. One was a kind of Cheaper by the Dozen fictionalized account of the large Turner family. The second was to be based on the life of her father: from hillbilly to sheriff to state representative, with many incidents about the prisoners in the jail. The third was to be a historical novel set in the time of President Jackson with an account of the Cherokee Indian removal. When Don first knew Lowney, she was working on a murder mystery whose main male character was a detective-philosopher. The text was filled with quotes from Eastern "wisdom" (Sackrider narrative).

Lowney could tell a story better than she could write it. When she turned to actual composition, her dialogue was most often flat, and there was no clear development of themes. She was always filled with ideas; they poured out every which way. Ideas were introduced, dropped, and replaced by others not always in any logical sequence. She was determined to be a writer, however, and worked at it for many years. Even though she was later to find success as an editor-critic, she continued to believe she was going to write a best-selling novel. Thus, in search of herself and in search of a career as writer, Lowney filled the early years of World War II working with the outcasts and renegades of Robinson. She corresponded with servicemen and entertained them when they were on leave, giving the impression that she was promiscuous though in fact she had little interest in sex.[2] Then James Jones entered her life.

2

James Jones: The Early Years of a Returning Soldier Who "Wants to Write"

James Ramon Jones, destined to be a central character in Lowney's life, was the son of Dr. Ramon Jones, dentist, and Ada Blessing Jones, housewife. He was born in Robinson, Illinois, on November 6, 1921. Seven miles from the Wabash River, the boundary with neighboring Indiana, Robinson is a typical midwestern small-town county seat, with a courthouse in the middle of the town square. It has always been somewhat different from the usual small town, however, because of the influence of oil money and the refinery, and there still are many fine homes in the city. The countryside is a mixture of rich prairie and bottom farmland, interspersed with abundant rolling woodlands, quite different from the flat farmland to the north.

Unlike Lowney Turner, James Jones was not born in a mansion, but his family lived in a comfortable house near the mansionlike home of his grandfather George W. Jones, a prosperous attorney who had once been sheriff of the county. The Jones family, Welsh in origin, had come to the States in the eighteenth century and had gradually moved westward. Early in his life, George W. Jones had been a farmer at Honey Creek, west of Robinson, the county seat of Crawford County. He came from a line of professional men and entered politics for a time, serving as sheriff of the county from 1886 to 1890, before apprenticing himself to a firm of local attorneys. He was admitted to the bar in 1892. His economic situation was greatly enhanced by the discovery of oil on his farm. The oil boom proved advantageous to both him and the community, for Robinson was home to the Lincoln Refinery (selling gas under the name of Linco), which was eventually acquired by the Ohio Oil Company.

George W. Jones was a teetotaler member of the Methodist Church, a man with a violent temper who dominated his wife and four sons. He demanded that his children attend Northwestern University and become professionals — two were to become doctors, two attorneys. He was proud to be a member of the Jones family and insisted that his sons live up to their family heritage. His authoritarian ways placed family members under psychological distress.

Ramon Jones, father of the future novelist, was slated by his father to be a doctor. Because Ramon wanted to leave Northwestern to be married, he received permission to become a dentist instead. He was a large man, popular, and a would-be poet. His father, too, was a writer, whose self-published book concerned a religious subject appropriate for an attorney — *The Trials of Christ: Were They Legal?* (MacShane 6–7).[1]

In 1908 Dr. Ramon Jones married the beautiful Ada Blessing, but it was not to be a happy marriage. Ada felt her family was more distinguished than the Joneses. She resented her wealthy father-in-law, whose dictatorial ways did not diminish over the years. She was a founding member of an elite social club in Robinson, but her life remained unfulfilled. Her firstborn, naturally named after his grandfather Jones but called Jeff, was born in 1910, but her second child was stillborn. During that pregnancy she gained a large amount of weight and was never afterward to solve her weight problem. She lost her beauty, and her health declined. She was diagnosed as a diabetic. In the midst of her personal turmoil she turned to Christian Science. Following Jim's birth, a daughter, Mary Ann, was born in 1925.

The Jones family life declined. Ada's frustrations no doubt added to her husband's unhappiness, and he began to drink heavily. His older brothers, too, were problem drinkers, and one brother took his own life while a student at Northwestern. Although more prosperous than the Turner family, the Joneses were certainly more troubled (MacShane 3–13). As James Jones wrote in an autobiographical sketch published in *Twentieth Century Authors:* "My father took to drink and my mother to religion" ("James Jones" 500). As a child and as an adult, Jim's sympathies lay with his father. In this respect he was like Lowney, who rejected her mother's religiosity and claims of social superiority and admired her father.

Jim was shy and small for his age, bookish, with weak eyes, so he had to wear glasses. He was caught in the turmoil of his parents' dysfunctional marriage. His older brother, Jeff, was athletic and outgoing, and he went away to college before the family economic situation became especially difficult. Jim and Mary Ann, on the other hand, were entangled in the family chaos, which intensified during the Great Depression.

His grandfather Jones, before his death in 1929, had invested heavily in the stock of Samuel Insull, the Chicago public utilities magnate. The Insull empire collapsed during the depression, and the Jones family suffered huge losses. The family fortune was wiped out. The colonial-style home was eventually acquired at a fire-sale price by Ramon's brother Charles Jones, who was executor of the estate. Later, some members of the family felt that Charlie had manipulated funds of the estate for his own advantage.

Dr. Ramon Jones eventually lost his own home nearby and had to move his family into a rented house. His dental practice declined precipitously. The loss of social prestige was especially hard for Ada Jones, but Jim was philosophical about the situation. In his autobiographical sketch, he wrote: "As a small boy I had accepted our family's social position without ever questioning it or even realizing it was there; I soon learned social prestige, while a very important thing, was still a very ephemeral one, and that if there is any permanency in this world at all, that is not it" ("James Jones" 501).

In school, Jim was bright, rebellious, cantankerous, and quick to confront schoolmates. Unlike his brother he was small and not well coordinated, so he did not excel in athletics. He was, however, already well read and was therefore bored in many of his classes. Literature classes, though, intrigued him, and he wrote imaginative themes, which made him even more unpopular with the high school in crowd. In his other classes, he made little effort to do well. He finished high school in 1939 with no prospects of college, for the family finances were still depressed.

Dr. Jones had served in World War I "and remembered it sentimentally" ("James Jones" 501). He recommended that his second son join the army. James Jones had no other viable prospects before him and agreed. First, however, he went to Findlay, Ohio, to visit his brother, Jeff, who worked in the Findlay office of the Ohio Oil Company, and the two discussed writing a novel together. Jim took a construction job for the summer and then went on the bum for a time. He hitchhiked to Canada and tried to join the Canadian army but was turned down. He had read Hemingway, and his desire to get into a foreign military service may have been influenced by World War I writers he had read. He returned to Robinson and, just after his eighteenth birthday, enlisted in the Army Air Corps. He was sent first to Chanute Field in east-central Illinois, where he discovered the food was terrible and that he was a successful gambler.

Soon after he entered the army, he began to experience burning when he urinated, accompanied by a painful discharge. He feared he had contracted gonorrhea, went on sick call, and was sent to the hospital for observation. By the time he wrote his brother in early December 1939, he was thinking of ways to use this experience:

> I had a chance to observe the men who had the "clap" as it is called in the army, and it gave me a good idea for our book. . . . It hinges on the attitude those guys in the clap ward have toward themselves and the

disease. It's all a big joke to them. They stand around a long sink and treat themselves with solutions. They laugh about it and make wisecracks about themselves. While I was being examined, I didn't know whether or not I had it or not [he did not]. I was so humiliated and ashamed at the aspect of being in that ward with those guys. (*To Reach Eternity* 5)

He then went on to give a plot outline of a proletarian novel in which workingmen are regularly killed on the job in a "money-mad" world that allows construction workers to be placed in physical jeopardy. The protagonist joins the army in desperation, but his "sensitive nature can't stand being herded around like cattle; treated like scum." After his enlistment is over he goes on the bum, but in desperation he joins the army once again. He contracts gonorrhea and is in the "clap" ward, where he feels himself unclean, his body "rotten to the core." He then jumps to his death (6).

During the summer of 1939, the two brothers had discussed the possibility of writing a novel together, and Jim was putting his new experiences directly into this proposed fiction, which was never written. The letter indicates, though the plot for the novel is proletarian, that Jones had the pride of his family, for he announced: "I . . . am better bred than any of these moronic sergeants" (6). He was already aware of the rigid caste system in the army, of the deep divide between officers and enlisted men, the arbitrary regulations, and the threat of being thrown into the guardhouse if one rebelled. He expressed his sexual frustrations to his brother: "I've been in quarantine up to now, and the only females I've seen have been at least 100 yds. off . . . with the exception of the theatre. There the officers' children . . . sit in the balcony. We common herd sit in the 'pit' as the rabble did in Shakespeare's day also" (4). He had learned a great deal in the month he had been in the army.

Jones sailed for Hawaii on December 18, 1939, by way of the Panama Canal and California—where he received a five-day pass and visited his mother's sister, Molly Haish, in Los Angeles. On his way back to Fort Mason where he was to board the troopship that would sail on to Hawaii, he met a girl who asked him to visit her. "I'll keep in touch with her," he wrote Jeff on February 1, 1940, "and if she isn't married by the time I get back to the States I'll look her up" (*To Reach Eternity* 9). Perhaps because it was expected of him, perhaps because of his romantic imagination, in the months to follow Jones was to allude often to his amatory exploits. He wrote his aunt Molly, in an undated letter penned soon after his arrival in Hawaii, about a Chinese girl: "I know she loves me. Her eyes shine when I kiss her. Her hair is as black as her eyes, if possible. It has a soft fragrance that makes my heart pound in my ears like a native drum" (MacShane 25). The love affairs and sexual conquests he bragged about seem to have been largely fanciful.

He was in a world of outcasts, sons of unemployed miners and factory workers who had little education and no prospects for a job during the depths of the depression. The army was a refuge, a relatively safe haven for the young renegades and castaways of American society. James Jones, a self-designated outcast since high school days, found a refuge in this stratified society of the old army.[2]

Jones was soon to be completely disenchanted with the Army Air Corps. His eyesight was poor, and he learned that he would never qualify as a pilot. The support units were held in low repute, he believed, and were treated badly. It was during this period of acute discontent at Hickam Field that he made a discovery that was to be a turning point in his life: "I stumbled upon the works of Thomas Wolfe, and his home life seemed so similar to my own, his feeling about himself so similar to mine about myself, that I realized I had been a writer all my life without knowing it or having written" ("James Jones" 501). He wrote Jeff in much the same vein on April 7, 1941: Wolfe was "the greatest writer that has lived. . . . I've always felt a hunger and unrest that nothing could satisfy" (*To Reach Eternity* 11, 12).

In September 1940, he transferred to the infantry, a branch of military service he considered more manly than the Air Corps. He went through basic training again and was stationed at Schofield Barracks, which he was to describe graphically in *From Here to Eternity*. He was still mostly a loner. He made a few friends such as Robert E. Stewart (who became the fictionalized Prewitt) and Frank Marshall (the scrawny Italian kid who became Friday in *From Here to Eternity*). Mostly, though, he kept to himself, using what time he had to write. He sent out stories and poems to popular magazines, but all were rejected. He continued to write, in spite of these disappointments.

He kept in touch with Jeff but seldom wrote his parents. His father wrote him on March 3, 1941, that his mother had died from congestive heart failure and diabetes. Jones professed to hate his mother, but he went on a three-day drunk in reaction to her death. In the letter, his father told him: "She missed your letters dreadfully and enjoyed them immensely whenever she did get one." Jeff wrote him that Ada Jones loved Jim more than her other two children. Whatever their problems in the past, Jones must have been moved by her letter to him on January 28, 1940: "Dad is feeling that long spell of drinking. He is having to build his business all over. I get scared sometimes, no home, and when that's gone [Dr. Jones's practice]. I wonder. I try to use my [Christian] science but I get scared anyway" (*To Reach Eternity* 10).

In his letter to Jeff about their mother's death, James Jones turned quickly to a discussion of Thomas Wolfe. Wolfe's mother had, in different ways, been as difficult as Mrs. Jones. She was turned into a memorable character in Wolfe's fiction. In Jones's paean to Wolfe, however, the mother figure is carefully excluded. Later, in his short stories such as "Just Like the Girl" and "The Tennis Game," Jones presented an only slightly fictionalized version of his mother in an entirely unfavorable light.

The next months were difficult for Jones. He was part of a corrupt, caste-ridden military life that paradoxically, because of its regimentation and male bonding, provided him with some security. As a common soldier, he was treated as a pariah, which blighted his social and sexual life. He had little money, and like most of the dogfaces he was forced to frequent the whorehouses or, as he remarked, "take care of himself" (MacShane 37).

Jones was lonely and frustrated when he wrote his brother in May 1941: "I'm working in the dark all the time. Whenever I do write something, that black, forbidding doubt is in me, making me wonder if I'm just some damned egotistical fool, or if I really have that spark of genius it takes to be a really great author like Wolfe. If only I had some way of knowing. If only some authority that knew would tell me I was good and had promise, then I'd be all right" (MacShane 38). It was this need for validation that was to lead him somewhat later to taking classes at the University of Hawaii, and eventually to Lowney Handy.

Jones's letters written during his army years in Hawaii show what a careful observer he was of the life around him. As an outsider, he had a unique interpretation of events, but he also participated in the life he was observing. The attack on Pearl Harbor gave him an unmatched opportunity to practice his participant-observer skills.

He was at breakfast the morning of December 7, 1941, when he heard rumblings, which he thought to be blasting. He rushed outside, as a Japanese plane flew over and strafed the area. He described the scene: "As he came abreast of us, he gave us a typically toothy grin and waved. . . . A white scarf streamed out behind his neck and he wore a white ribbon around his helmet just above the goggles, with a red spot in the center of his forehead. I would later learn that this ribbon was a *hachimaki*, the headband worn by medieval samurai when going into battle" (*WW II* 16, 25).

Jones spent the morning carrying messages for officers. Since there was fear of more bombing and strafing at Schofield Barracks and of an immediate invasion of the island, troops, including Jones, were dispersed, Jones and his comrades being sent to guard the area around Makapuu Point.[3] Later, he was to re-create his feelings, his sense of history, as they were being evacuated from the barracks: "I remember thinking . . . that none of our lives would ever be the same, that a social, even a cultural watershed had been crossed which we could never go back over, and I wondered how many of us would survive to see the end results. I wondered if I would. I had just turned twenty, the month before" (*WW II* 25). While Company F was guarding the beaches, Jones received a letter from Jeff telling him Dr. Jones had taken his own life.

In a controlled but emotional letter, Jones wrote Jeff words that must have been seared in his mind, key words that would reappear in the titles of his first and last published novels: *eternity and whistle*. After he read the letter, he sat on his bed, smoking. "Sometimes the air is awfully clear here," he wrote

Jeff. "You can look off to sea and see the soft, warm raggedy roof of clouds stretching on and on and on. It almost seems as if you can look right on into eternity." He went down to the beach where he smashed a crab into the sand: "Then the sea rolled up again and back again. In a little while there was no mark upon the sand at all and the crab was nowhere to be seen. The sea rolled on, timeless in its vastness, and did not seem to care that a crab had been killed there. . . . For life, just like the sea, has never lost a battle yet. Perhaps it has been thwarted for a time, but it always comes back in the last quarter to score again, for the game has no final whistle. It ends only when you quit or cannot fight some more" (*To Reach Eternity* 17–18).

Jones knew his father had been weak, but then and later he defended his father's actions, to the displeasure of his uncle Charles Jones. He put part of the blame for the suicide on the provincialism of Robinson, though it seems obvious that much of the blame should be placed at the doorstep of his autocratic grandfather, George W. Jones, who had attempted to control his son's life.

During the spring of 1942, after it became clear that the Japanese were not going to invade Hawaii, Jones was allowed to enroll in a course in composition and American literature at the University of Hawaii. His rhetoric teacher, Laura Schwartz, and his literature professor, Carl Stroven, were both impressed by his writing. These two were the first to give a professional opinion that he had the talents and the command of subject matter to become a writer. Much of what he wrote at that time was influenced by, and closely akin to, Thomas Wolfe's writing. But this was not always the case. In a paper reviewing Stephen Crane's *The Red Badge of Courage* submitted on October 12, 1942, Jones wrote a remarkable critique, utilizing his own experiences and including a dramatic account of the strafing of Schofield Barracks and his own assessment of cowardice and courage (*James Jones Reader* 387–93). Jones had already experienced war when he wrote his war novels; Crane had not.

Schwartz and Stroven recognized Jones's abilities as a writer, and this gave him some confidence, but what he did not have, what nobody could give him, was foreknowledge that he would survive the war and become a professional writer. In an undated manuscript, he wrote, "I might be dead in a month, which would mean that I would never learn how to say and never get said those things which proved I had once existed somewhere" (*To Reach Eternity* 24). Paradoxically, he knew that every combat soldier "must make a compact with himself or with Fate that he is lost. Only then can he function as he ought to function, under fire. He knows and accepts beforehand that he's dead, although he may still be walking around for a while." He had to admit "that his name is already written down in the rolls of the already dead" (*WW II* 54).

It was with great foreboding that Jones went into combat. He arrived at Guadalcanal on December 30, 1942, where bloody battles had already been and were still to be fought. The conditions on the island were terrible. The troops suffered from tropical disease such as malaria and dengue fever and from the psychological numbing caused by witnessing the death and mutilation of their comrades.

Jones gave a graphic description of the horrors of the battlefield in *The Thin Red Line*, which many consider one of the best war novels ever written. Much earlier, he had written a poem, "The Hill They Call the Horse," about the fight for a complex of hills on Guadalcanal called "The Galloping Horse." Jones was wounded in this battle. The poem begins:

> I am in a hospital, and it is the middle of the night.
> I cannot sleep.

The autobiographical persona is in turmoil. The scenes of that battle come to him, his dead comrades pass before him:

> For across the crest they come
> In solitary line
> As I last saw them . . .
> They pass by me with stumbling tread,
> And each looks at me reproachfully and sadly:
> They died; I lived. They resent my luck.
> They cannot see that I am not the lucky one.
> As they pass I see them as I saw them last:
> George Creel—
> A little string of brains hanging down between his eyes;
> Joe Donnicci—
> His eyes big behind his glasses and a gaping hole where once had
>   been his ear
> Young Shelley—
> Balls shot away and holding in his guts that pooch out between his
>   fingers. . . .
> The line goes on—for there are many more.
>
> (*To Reach Eternity* 32–35)

He knew, by the end of the poem, that he would need to revisit that place of carnage, and this is exactly what he did when he wrote *The Thin Red Line*, although the return trip was imagined rather than actual. The poem captures the "swirling wisps of madness and of pain" in the battle and in the mind of the poet.

Three events that were to change his life occurred on Guadalcanal. The first was that he killed a Japanese soldier, a scene dramatized in the novel *The Thin Red Line*. He had gone into the jungle to defecate, and while his pants were around his ankles a Japanese soldier, bayonet in hand, charged him. They engaged in hand-to-hand combat, and Jones finally killed the soldier. Only then could he see how emaciated the man was, and in his pocket he found a photograph of the man's wife and child. The sensitive young soldier from Robinson, Illinois, was repelled by his actions, by the consequences of his actions, and he told his commanding officer that he would not fight again (MacShane 56). To the living nightmares of his wounded and dying comrades, Jones added the ghost of the Japanese soldier he had killed.

The second important event was that he was wounded. He described it in a letter to Jeff:

> I wasn't hit very badly—a piece of shrapnel went thru my helmet and cut a nice little hole in the back of my head . . . I don't know what happened to my helmet; the shell landed close to me and when I came to, the helmet was gone. The concussion . . . must have broken the chin-strap and torn it off my head. It also blew my glasses off my face. I never saw them again, either, but I imagine they are smashed to hell . . . it bothers you a lot to know you can't see well and that any minute some sniper you should have seen but couldn't is liable to cut you down.

He decided that training and precautions have nothing to do with survival in battle. It is "largely a matter of luck." In his letter, he indicated that it was likely he would be killed, and he asked Jeff to write the book they had discussed. He wanted Jeff to "put into the book the promise that I had" (*To Reach Eternity* 25–26, 27).

The third important event was that he was removed from the battlefields of Guadalcanal and, as it happened, from all future battles of World War II. His right ankle had been giving him trouble since he injured it playing football at Schofield Barracks. One day on Guadalcanal, after the fighting was over, he was walking with a first sergeant and turned his ankle and was told to report for medical care. Jones thought the medics would not pay much attention, he feared he would be considered a malingerer. The first sergeant told him, "If it's as bad as what I saw, you got no business in the infantry." All his friends urged him to get medical help, to get shipped out and away from upcoming battles. He was evacuated to a naval hospital in the New Hebrides, his ankle was operated on, and he was sent back to the United States by way of New Zealand (*WW II* 137–39; MacShane 58–59).

Jones arrived in San Francisco on May 19, 1943, and was soon sent to Kennedy General Hospital in Memphis, Tennessee, where the condition of many of the evacuees was grim: amputees, blind men, some terribly disfigured.

Jones had come from the horrors of battle to a hospital full of the lingering effects of worldwide military activities. He was unhinged. He had been drinking heavily for some time. There had been binges in Hawaii when he was under great stress, such as the time after his mother's death. The Americans on Guadalcanal had brewed their own rot-gut, and Jones had sought what oblivion the foul-tasting stuff offered him. He had gone on drunks while on leave in San Francisco, as he was being evacuated to Tennessee. Once he was on the mend, he was given passes to go into Memphis, where he continued to drink heavily. Some of the wounded soldiers, including Jones, took rooms at the local hotels where compliant local women provided sexual favors for the returning heroes. It was one of the most difficult periods of his life and provided the basis for significant portions of his last novel, *Whistle*.

In August 1943, he was discharged from the hospital and declared fit to return to duty. He had expected to be discharged from the army, and he immediately went off on a drunk. He then went AWOL and left for Robinson where he stayed with his uncle and aunt, Charles and Sadie Jones, who now owned the family mansion that had once belonged to George W. Jones. His conventional uncle was hard-pressed to understand his psychologically damaged nephew.

Before he actually saw his nephew again, his uncle Charlie at first had expressed sympathy for his nephew's desires to become a writer. Charlie wrote: "I expect you are right in saying that I regard you more as the kid who left here 4 years ago, rather than the individual you have developed into through those years. I had heard from Jeff that you wanted to write, but I never knew, or had any chance to know, what talent you have along those lines." He went on to say that he believed he had been thinking too much about the practical things, about how his nephew would make a living. Still, he did not discourage his wounded relative: "Your idea of going to school to prepare yourself to write is a good one. . . . So more power to your old power house" (June 19, 1943, UIS).

The good relations between the two were not to last long. Instead of being discharged in early November, as he had hoped, Jones was assigned to Camp Campbell in Kentucky. Then he went AWOL and arrived in Robinson by bus. At the time Jones had vague socialist leanings, at least he was suspicious of those with money, and there were hard feelings in the family about his uncle Charlie living in the family mansion. Charlie's wife, Sadie, was originally from Tennessee, and she had southern charm and a southern accent. Jones was still in great psychological distress in November 1943, now thinking of a novel to be called *They Shall Inherit the Laughter*, fearful that reassignment in the army would mean his return to one of the fighting fronts and almost certain death.

On his first day back in Robinson, November 5, 1943, he saw childhood friends and that night took his friend Annis Skaggs to the high school football game. The next day, November 6, was his twenty-second birthday, and his uncle Charlie gave a party for him at the local Elks Club. Jones had too much to drink and made a speech promising to write a book about the people there, exposing their "conniving souls and sneaky love affairs" (MacShane 74). Annis drove him around for a time, but she was unable to get him into the mansion herself and had to call on Charlie for help. Annis believed that Jones had put on an act deliberately to offend Charlie and the citizens of Robinson at the Elks Club, but it should be remembered just how confused and psychologically troubled Jones was, and his motivation is not entirely clear.

There were more troubles the next day, November 7. He was still drinking heavily that night, and he passed out at the Mission Tea Room, a local restaurant. Annis had to drive him home. Apparently later that month Jim again drank too much and a policeman drove him to the Jones mansion. This time Charlie would not take him in and had him jailed. Jones never forgave his uncle who was, he believed, "trying to break me thru fear and humiliation" (MacShane 74).

It was one of these afternoons, perhaps November 6 (not November 3, the date given in Whipple, as he did not arrive in Robinson until November 5) that James Jones met Lowney Handy. Jones's Aunt Sadie, more understanding of her distressed nephew than his uncle was, had gone to see Lowney for help and told the story of the wayward Jones boy.

"He thinks he wants to write," Sadie told Lowney.

"Oh, my God, no," said Lowney. "Not a writer!" (Whipple 144).

Whipple, in his article, explained Lowney's reaction: she had taken a novel to New York and had had an interview with an editor, who looked at it quickly and declined it. "What he really meant, though," she reported, "was that I was a frustrated, childless, middle-aged woman trying to find something to do, and that I had better go home and find something else" (144). This story may have been exaggerated, for Lowney in the interview with Whipple (at the time of the success of *From Here to Eternity*) was clearly shaping events. There is essential truth in the story, however. Lowney's fiction was poorly done and would have been turned down by publishers, and she was clearly frustrated in the fall of 1943. Whipple summarized Lowney's feelings after her disastrous trip to see a New York publisher: "She had gone home carrying in her heart a bitter determination to show them all someday. But anybody who had anything to do with writing made her very angry this soon after her experience." Sadie knew, however, that Lowney could not "say no to anyone in trouble" (144). Arrangements were made for Jim to meet Lowney.

3
The Beginnings of *From Here to Eternity* and of the Handy Colony

You should have seen him then," Lowney told Whipple about her first meeting with Jones. "He swaggered; he wore dark glasses; he even asked me to read his poetry aloud. He had obviously come over for a free drink. Then he saw my books. We have books everywhere in the house. . . . Jim got out of his chair and began to take out the books. He flipped through them and plopped them back as if he were gulping down what they had in them" (144). Lowney was clearly putting Jones in the tradition of Thomas Wolfe, who read his way quickly and compulsively through the Harvard library. "So I asked him if he'd like to see my writing room. It's lined with books. He went from shelf to shelf. Then he picked out a couple and sat down on the floor with them, and I might as well have been in the next country. I just stood there and looked at him. The chip on the shoulder was gone. The poor guy. The poor lost guy" (147).

Lowney's version of her first meeting with Jim may have been good publicity, but it was more than somewhat less than truthful. According to Lowney, "The aunt had to remind Jim it was time to leave. A few days later he was back, and this time Harry was there. The three talked on and on. After Jim left that evening, the Handys made the decision they have stuck by ever since. They decided to take Jim into their household" (Whipple 147). On November 8, however, Jones wrote in his notebook that he had spent the day in bed with Lowney. By November 11 she had seen some of his writing, and because she was impressed with it, "she subjected herself to me; she made herself my disciple in everything from writing to love" (MacShane 77). It is clear that Jones must have met Harry on one of his visits, for he described Harry as "a wonderful guy; he knew Lowney and I made love all day but he didn't mind — rather he understood — and was glad" (76–77). Jones's diary entries show that he misunderstood or fantasized about his relationship with Lowney. Lowney was undoubtedly convinced Jim had potential as a writer, but she certainly did not then or later subject herself to him. It is probably true, however, that she had told Harry she was having an affair with the young soldier. Lowney and Harry had been going their separate ways for years, but they insisted on keeping their marriage intact.

Jim's antagonism toward his uncle Charlie continued, and he was beginning to move his allegiance to Lowney, who appeared to revel in her new role. She wrote Charlie Jones that Jim came to her house "because the sort of people I gather around me are his kind. . . . He wants to turn his life upside down to get away from all that being told of the past four years. For all artists are Bohemian, and Jim will be a great artist if nothing devastating happens." She told Charlie rather cryptically about her new role of teacher-editor: "I . . . have a job to do" (November 23, 1943, UIS).

According to Whipple, Harry and Lowney "set out to rehabilitate" Jim. "The first job was to get him out of the army" (147). This meant he had to return to his base. He was not court-martialed upon his return to Camp Campbell in Kentucky. Instead, after a sympathetic warrant officer adjusted his orders to hide the unauthorized leave, he was sent on maneuvers prior to being shipped overseas once again, this time to Europe. Jim was not completely recovered physically, he was in a precarious psychological state, and his desire to become a writer had been validated by Lowney's enthusiasm for his fiction. He was afraid he would not survive another tour of duty in a war zone.

Once again he went AWOL, this time over the Thanksgiving holiday, and he stayed drunk for three days. Again he returned to Camp Campbell, where he was reduced in rank to private. He was transferred to the 842 Quarter Master Gas and Supply Company, where the work was monotonous and boring. He was drawn ever closer to the Handys and requested a transfer to George Field (nearer Robinson) in order to be closer to Lowney. Charlie wrote Jim's commanding officer suggesting that the transfer be denied. Jim saw his uncle's letter, and on January 29, 1944, wrote him a long letter breaking family ties. He felt his uncle had humiliated him, and he now needed Lowney and Harry more than ever (*To Reach Eternity* 75).

His work was satisfactory, and on March 1, 1944, Jim was promoted to sergeant, but he still went AWOL, and in May he packed his belongings and left for Indianapolis, where he worked on a novel he called *They Shall Inherit the Laughter*. Lowney tracked him down and convinced him to return to Camp Campbell. Upon his return he was sent to the stockade, where he saw some of the brutality described in the stockade scenes in *From Here to Eternity*. Depressed and suicidal, he was transferred to the prison ward in the hospital. He wrote his brother about the interview with a psychiatrist: "I told . . . that I am genius (altho they probably won't believe that); that if they attempt to send me overseas again, I'll commit suicide; that if I don't get out of the army I'll either go mad or turn into a criminal . . . ; that all I want to do is write." The diagnosis of the doctors: Jones had a "psychoneurosis, mixed anxiety and compulsive types with schizoid trends" (MacShane 67–69).

In the meantime Lowney was working to get Jim discharged from the army. She probably used her political connections. The army doctors did recognize his mental and physical problems, and Lowney constantly badgered "everyone in the Army" for his release (Whipple 147). Jones received an honorable discharge on July 6, 1944, "for disability in line of duty and not due to his own misconduct" (MacShane 70). He received a small disability pension; his only other income was a few dollars each month in royalties from a family-owned oil well. His uncle was unsympathetic. Jim's future would have been bleak had the Handys not taken him in.

After his discharge, Jim paid his literary respects to Thomas Wolfe by going to Asheville, North Carolina, to visit the Wolfe home and sites connected with *Look Homeward, Angel*. He then returned to Robinson and moved in with the Handys, first staying upstairs where Lowney also had a bedroom. Harry's bedroom was downstairs.

Jim worked on *They Shall Inherit the Laughter* for the next few months. His subject was the return of American veterans to the Midwest. The bitter autobiographic hero, Johnny Carter, is "adopted" by an older woman, unfortunately named Corny Marion, whose yes-saying is based on Emersonian and American transcendentalist ideas and Oriental mysticism, beliefs cherished by Lowney. Steven R. Carter, in his perceptive study *James Jones: An American Literary Orientalist Master*, wrote:

> Jones made his borrowings from Christianity (occult or otherwise), transcendentalism, Orientalism, Platonism, theosophy, and Lowney Handy his own when he shaped his philosophy and sharpened his creative writing. . . . Moreover, his eclectic philosophy, composed from borrowings and given vitality and originality by the experiences, character, and highly personal revision of its creator, much as Emerson absorbed his borrowings and gave the world transcendentalism, became the "unsevered thread" that Jones wanted to hold his work together. (34)[1]

Jim was too close to his material to shape his novel, and he recognized his need for more education. He was accepted at New York University, where Thomas Wolfe had once taught, and he began classes there in the spring of 1945 (MacShane 77).

Jim had an introduction to an agent, Maxwell Aley, and actually stayed with the Aleys for a few days before he found a room in the city. Aley read the novel and recommended extensive revisions, which angered Jim, for Lowney had praised it highly. Her own writings were almost formless, and her ear for dialogue in her stories was then faulty. Her criticism of that novel was surely amateurish, but she was undoubtedly praising his writing, regardless of its quality, to keep up his morale. Distressed, Jim took the novel to Maxwell Perkins, then the most distinguished editor in the United States, known to all literate readers of American fiction as Scribner's editor for the works of Thomas Wolfe, Ernest Hemingway, and F. Scott Fitzgerald. Jim talked his way into Perkins's office, spoke to the editor about his desire to be a writer and about his experiences in the army, and left his manuscript (MacShane 77–78). The two adjourned to the Ritz Bar. Perkins did not read the novel at that time but assigned it to two other editors, who were not enthusiastic. Perkins, however, had been impressed with Jones and then went through the novel himself. He wrote Jim's agent, Aley: "It is a serious attempt to do a big piece of work and the author has the temperament and the emotional projection of a writer." He went on to say, "We do not feel however that *They Shall Inherit the Laughter* quite comes off as a novel, nor does it turn out to be anything for which we could make you an offer" (*To Reach Eternity* 48).

Perkins did recommend extensive changes, and Jim spent a considerable amount of time in his remaining months in New York working over his novel. He was a good student at New York University, but he was lonely and asked Lowney to join him in New York at the end of the spring term. He decided not to continue college. It was a happy time for the two lovers, and after a short time they left Manhattan for Florida.

Jim's manuscript was overblown and awkward in many places and needed major changes. He wrote Perkins from Marathon, Florida, on November 20, 1945, that he was in the last phases of preparing his manuscript for resubmission, having rewritten chapters several times. He concluded, "I am offering it to you now first, partially because I still have a soft spot for the character Tom Wolfe drew from you, but mainly because I feel I owe you a debt of gratitude for not publishing the book as it was when I submitted it" (*To Reach Eternity* 49).

Jim was perpetually short of money during the months after he left the army. Lowney and Harry provided him with room and board in Robinson or Florida, but he had little spending money. His disability check was less than fifty dollars a month, and only small sums came from the oil well royalties. He wrote his aunt, Molly Haish, on December 13, 1945, "I've been doing a little commercial fishing both in the Gulf and the Atlantic, when I run short of dough. I go out with a man who lives next door who owns a 34 ft. launch.

It's fascinating, and a good break now and then from writing too hard. I made $20 one night" (*To Reach Eternity* 52–53).

In the same letter, he told his aunt he was looking into religion. He reminded her that he had earlier been antireligious because of his experiences with churches in Robinson. "But now," he wrote, "I've learned that if a man can disregard and forget the churches, that there's a tremendous amount of knowledge in the Bible." He went on to say that he was reading the works of Paul Brunton. Carter discusses Jim's interest in theosophy and occultism at length. Lowney had a large collection of occult books and loaned them freely; Jim read many of those books in her library and, like the American Transcendentalists, chose certain parts eclectically. He was drawn to the theory of reincarnation and to a belief in the oversoul. These ideas were in the American grain during the middle of the nineteenth century, for they are to be found in the works of Emerson, Thoreau, Whitman, and several others.

Jim was unable to keep his self-imposed deadline of January 1, 1946, for completing the revisions of *They Shall Inherit the Laughter,* and he wrote Perkins a letter of explanation. In a fatherly fashion, Perkins responded on January 7, 1946, that since writing is not an exact science, the time it takes cannot be calculated. He advised Jones to send the manuscript when the retyping was completed. Jim sent the manuscript on January 17.

Three weeks later, he had received no response, and on February 10, 1946, from his brother's home in Tallahassee, he wrote a letter of inquiry. In that long letter he sketched his ideas for several other novels; from the text it is clear he had in mind *From Here to Eternity, The Thin Red Line,* and *Whistle,* and that at this stage of his thinking he believed he could cover all this material in one novel (*To Reach Eternity* 55–56).

Jim's writing career might have been entirely different had he not told Perkins, "I have always wanted to do a novel on the Peacetime army." He then sketched the idea of *From Here to Eternity,* using the actual names of soldiers he had known (later the names were changed — Wendson becomes Warden and Stewart is presented as Prewitt):

> (Stewart is an old friend in the army, Wendson is a former 1st/Sgt of mine. I would use both in the same company.) Draw Stewart's life in army, his intense personal pride, his six months on stockade rockpile rather than admit he was wrong and accept company punishment when he felt he was right in his actions. The small man standing on the edge of the ocean shaking his fist, the magnificent gesture, both Wendson and Stewart completely fearless (unloved men, yet forced to prove to themselves that they can get along without love, because they have never had honesty or love, insist that they neither miss them or want them. (*To Reach Eternity* 56–57)

Perkins telegraphed Jim on February 15, 1946: "Would you consider payment five hundred now for option on Stewart novel and setting aside *Inherit Laugh-*

ter for reasons I'll write? Some further payment to be made after we read say first fifty thousand words. Wish to cooperate but have more faith in second novel and have further revisions to propose for *Laughter*" (60).

Jim had found another authority who believed in him. Lowney had been telling him he had great abilities as a writer, and now Thomas Wolfe's editor had faith in his potential. Jim did not seem to notice that Lowney had been wrong in her high praise of *Laughter*, and her influence on him and his work grew. After all, she had been the first to believe in him and encourage him.

Perkins wrote Jim a long, considerate letter on February 19, 1946, giving reasons for not accepting *Laughter*. He felt that the public would not be interested in the subject—the return of a bitter veteran—and that the novel would insult military people and civilians. It might be more acceptable in a few years, he said. It was not to be; Jim returned to the subject in *Some Came Running*, but the earlier text was abandoned. Brilliant editor that he was, Perkins knew how to encourage the young man whose first novel had once again been rejected: "As for the book you are now to do, it seemed to us from what you said, that you saw something truly important, and that you were right in your interpretation of the nature of that type of man, and that he had never been portrayed in a way to make him understandable. There is something widely appealing in him, too, and something tragic. I hope therefore, that you will go forward with enthusiasm in the writing" (*To Reach Eternity* 60).

Perkins kept on encouraging the young writer. He wrote Jim on March 27, 1946, urging him to keep a notebook. He suggested that he make notes on cards and then classify the notes under key words. "I think," Perkins wrote, "if a writer did that for ten years, all those memories would come back to him . . . and he would have an immense fund to draw upon. One can write nothing unless it is, in some sense, out of one's life—that is, out of oneself" (*To Reach Eternity* 60–61). Jim did make notes about the characters to appear in *From Here to Eternity* (apparently these are the ones published in *The James Jones Reader*). The notes make it clear that *From Here to Eternity* was to be "the story of Prewitt. His story must be a tragedy, as the army is a tragedy" (*James Jones Reader* 394). Jim put in his notes personal views that were reflected in the plotting and character development in the novel:

> The meaning of the army for me is one of personal degradation, a degradation that is inescapable once a man is hooked, a degradation rising directly out of the system of caste and privilege and arbitrary authority. . . . *The most logical way to handle this then, is to show a man caught by the army.* Prewitt. He is forced in by economic forces and once in cannot escape without sacrificing his self-respect and integrity, which he refuses to do. . . . *I assert it is impossible to escape this degradation unless a man allows his own moral nature to be corrupted.* (394; original italics)

In his early notes for the novel, it is clear that part of the "arid hopelessness" of enlisted men came from the lack of women. He was explicit about the homosexual subplots of the novel-in-progress: "*Intensive sexual frustration, from lack of women* (plus lack of money) *which drives a lot of men into abortive sexuality*—usually with queers downtown" (395, 397).

The notes are extensive, giving explicit details about the characters of Prew, Warden, Stark, Holmes. Karen Holmes is mentioned only in passing: "Deliberately, with malice aforethought, Warden decides to seduce Holmes's wife in retaliation. *Irony:* they both fall in love." Lorene, the ice-maiden prostitute, is not mentioned in the notes (400).

Jim returned to Robinson and settled into the Handy household once again, working on the novel that was to become *From Here to Eternity*. On May 27, 1946, he wrote Perkins that he had completed 173 pages. After Perkins read those chapters, he wrote Jim that he had included too much explanatory material. (Lowney, too, in her writing never seemed to avoid this problem, but she was developing her editorial skills and did help Jim.) Perkins also had a suggestion that Jim did try to follow: "When you come to revise, you must try to make the action, and the talk (which is a form of action) tell it all, or almost all" (MacShane 83).

Alienated from his uncle Charlie, Jim was drawn more and more into the Handys' orbit. He was on friendly though somewhat remote terms with Harry, but life with Lowney had its high and low spots. At her best she was charming, loving, and provocative. She was also authoritarian and quick to make judgments; she appeared to be a person completely in control but was actually nervous and overly emotional, sometimes making events spin out of control. She was quixotic in many ways but single-minded in her belief that Jim was going to be a major writer. He often spoke of himself in this period of his life as being oversexed, and she was willing for a time to fulfill his sexual needs, though she took little pleasure in sex (MacShane 76–77). Lowney and Harry unofficially adopted Jim and built a room and bath on the back of their house for him. It was not that Harry wanted Jim as a son; he wanted to please Lowney, to do whatever she wished.

Jim's letters to Perkins were long and detailed, and it is clear that he was attempting to follow the advice he was receiving. Lowney, too, was constantly reading his material, commenting on it, making suggestions. Her own abilities as a critic and editor were also improved by Perkins's letters. Jim needed help; he was still in psychological pain, restless, often unfocused, and Lowney became his warden, attempting to control him and rehabilitate him as if he were a prisoner. She was also a compulsive conversationalist, and she filled Jim with stories of the Turners in Kentucky. She told her friend and agent, Ned Brown (and undoubtedly Jim): "My father's people were all killers" (February 21, 1957, UIS). John Turner appears in the novel as Prew's uncle; the Prewitt family is given to violence just as the Turners were, just as Cash Clay was. Perhaps more important, Jim was drawing on the situation in the Handy household: he transfers several events in Lowney's life to Karen Holmes, especially her being infected with gonorrhea and the subsequent hysterectomy. He shows Karen and Captain Holmes going their own way, each having their own affairs.

Lowney also bought books, unsystematically, but she did buy books, read them, and made them available to Jim. Some books she certainly encouraged him to read: books on the occult by Paul Brunton, works on theosophy by Madame Blavatsky and Annie Besant, and books on dietary and health reform. These books did have a long-term effect on Jim, as Carter shows.

To the outer Robinson world, this ménage à trois was scandalous, but Harry, Lowney, and Jim lived together for many years, largely ignoring the gossip. In truth Harry and Lowney lived mostly separate lives, and they lived in harmony; Jim and Harry also lived in (distant) harmony. Jim and Lowney, however, did not always live in harmony. Lowney was intent upon controlling his life, in making him focus on the writing of *Eternity*, writing that was often slow and painful. She was a stern mother, a reluctant lover, and an autocratic teacher. At times she declared she was sacrificing her own writing in order to help Jim; at other times she worked at stories or a novel and believed she was going to be successful. Some days in the Handy household were placid, but others were tension-filled with charges and recriminations: He wrote about "Rebellion-Frustration" in his notebook:

> How Lowney and I fought over her story in the final copying. And finally she said to hell with it, it doesn't mean that much to me, I'll just not finish it.
> And I said, "Thats not true."
> And she looked at me and said, "It don't mean a *fuck* to me."
> "Thats a lot of *shit*," I said. "And you know it."
> "All right," she said, as if that meant something, "I'll *prove* it to you." And got up and walked out.
> I wanted to beat my fists against the wall with the frustration IN ME. I lay on the floor with head in my hands, but in the back of my mind was the picture of her coming back and finding me in this obviously tragic position. But she did not come back. I wandered around the room and went outside and came back in and told myself it didnt mean anything to me, it was none of my worry, and finally I went out front, where she was sitting languidly indifferently on the steps smelling two flowers, a purple iris and a white one of some kind, and I knew that she was calculating her attitude for me to see it, just as I had calculated mine before.
> I was very angry and piqued because I had to go outside, instead of her having to come inside to me, and thought how it always happens that way, it was always me who had to make the first overtures.
> But I told her it was stupid to do that, and reminded her of how I would use to threaten to tear up my writing when I got mad and disgusted or hurt.

"Are you going to finish this story?" I said.

"I really just dont think its worth it, Jim," she said, with an air of great put-upon tiredness, the supreme indifference of worn-outness.

"Then I think I just wont finish my novel," I said.

"Well," she said, "thats up to you, isn't it?"

"Its the same thing," I said. "As your not finishing the story."

Both of us had apparently forgotten all about the original purpose, as she propounded it, the chance of getting $2000. This had become a battle between the wills, sort of.

"I mean it," I said. "If you dont finish this story, I wont finish my book. I mean it."

"All right," she said with great exhaustion. "All right. I'll come back in a little while. Just leave me alone a while. Please, just leave me alone."

I went back inside, but before I went I heard a small plaintive whistle repeated at continuous intervals from somewhere near the high-bush-cranberry, and began looking for it. "Its a thrush," she said, still with this great tiredness but not nearly so much now because of her great instinct of protection for the thrush. "He's right at your feet. Dont move or you'll scare him." (*To Reach Eternity* 61–62)

Jim at times also threw material away. Lowney often told the story about Jim's tossing out chapter 2 of *Eternity* (the chapter containing a biographical sketch of Prewitt and his Kentucky family, much of it drawn from stories Lowney had told about her family and her uncle John). Lowney retrieved the chapter and convinced Jim it was perfect just as it was. Jim trusted her, and the chapter was never rewritten. Don Sackrider heard Lowney tell this story in Jim's presence, and Jim never refuted her account (Sackrider narrative).

Tensions between Lowney and Jim flared and subsided. And as Lowney worked with Jim, page by page, her editorial skills increased, and she began to seek other students. Don Sackrider, who had grown up in Robinson, was brought into her orbit.

Although Robinson was and is a small town of about five thousand, Don had never heard of Lowney Handy, although her younger brother Earl had recently married his mother's good friend Belva. The Handys were Robinson society, his mother said. And Don pictured a woman with red nails and beauty parlor hair, middle aged or older, a bridge player. He was seventeen that spring of 1947 and would be graduating from high school in another week.

"She's a writer," his mother explained, "and Belva was talking to Lowney about us and said you wanted to be a writer, too."

Don did not really want to be a writer as much as he wanted to be an actor. He had worked hard the summer of 1946 and saved his money in order not to have to work after school his senior year. Free from work, he could be in the school plays. He had just played the only male part in the drama club production of *Ladies in Retirement*.

"Hap Handy," Don's mother said (calling Harry by the name Belva must have used), "is very high up out at the refinery. If you want a summer job there it could not hurt to know them." Don's mother rarely pushed him to do anything, but this time she did.

"I'm going to California, Polly," he stated and restated. He wanted to see movieland. He called his mother Polly, and though she did not exactly like it, she never instructed him not to.

Don's parents had divorced when he was seven. His father had disappeared one night, and his whereabouts were unknown for several months. A local couple, Nita and Pete, had wanted to adopt Don; his father's brother wanted to adopt Don and his brother; but Polly was horrified at the thought of giving up her sons and did not do so. The Sackriders had little money. Polly was a single parent. His grandmother and aunt had a washing and ironing business at home. Nita and Pete did take him on trips and give him presents his mother could not afford. Pete, before he died (when Don was eleven), had wanted to send Don to medical school.

Polly was more insistent: "But she [Lowney] has called again. She really wants to meet you."

Don was out of school until graduation. Polly, home from work on her lunch hour, called Lowney to say Don would come that afternoon. He had a pleasant mile-long walk; spring flowers were blooming in the yards and trees were newly leafed. Number 202 West Mulberry was an unpretentious house with a picket fence in front. He could not find anything that looked like a main door or a front door, and there was no answer to the door where he knocked. He decided with a sigh of relief that no one was home, and he would be spared this unwanted meeting.

"Only white folks use that door," came a voice from a door near the garage. "I'm back here," the woman's voice rang out.

When he saw her, he confirmed she was middle-aged, for her hair was salt-and-pepper gray, but she did not fit his notion of the bridge club set. Her voice, although a little high, was full of warmth and charm.

"Come in and welcome. You must be Donald."

"I'm Don Sackrider," he said, as she pulled him into the house, into a kitchen with a big round oak table covered with a red checkered cloth.

"Mrs. Handy?" he asked, for she was not how he had expected.

"Call me Lowney. Make yourself cool and sit here in the kitchen." Her voice, Don recognized, had a southern lilt to it. His family all spoke straight Illinois Midwest.

The kitchen seemed dark after the walk in the bright afternoon sun, but her eyes were flashing and brilliant in her tanned, pleasant face. Her salt-and-pepper hair was straight but combed to curl under. Her teeth were white and strong. She often bragged that she could crack hickory nuts with her teeth. Her smile was radiant.

Don sat at the table and was given coffee. Like an adult, he thought.

"Hobo coffee," she said, pointing to the big enamel pot. "I make it strong but never boiled 'cause that brings out the bitter oils. Then add hot water." She kept a kettle on a low burner.

"Thank you, Mrs. Handy," he said, and she told him again to call her Lowney. He kept saying Mrs. Handy because he was unsure about the pronunciation of "Lowney." Was it *Loh-ney* or *Lau-ney?* He couldn't quite remember how she said this strange name. (He would eventually learn it was *Loh-ney*, with a long *o* and a silent *w*.)

"Now tell me about Don Sackrider," she said.

Is this lady really as interested in hearing about me as she appears to be? he thought.

She sat with her head cocked and expectant.

"I graduate from high school next week. I'm going to Indiana State in the fall, but I'm going to California this summer," he told her.

"And you want to be a writer? You want to write, I understand."

Don nodded. "But I want to act. I want to be an actor."

He did not expect her response: "That's wonderful. You can do both."

He was impressed by her enthusiasm. She was not silent and frowning, as most people in Robinson when he mentioned his ambition. He told her about saving his money to be free to act in plays his senior year, about traveling to New York by himself the summer he was fifteen to see a Broadway play, about going to Cuba during the Christmas vacation of his junior year.

He was aware at this time that in this small town they had never heard of each other, had not even seen each other. They moved in different circles. The Handys were Elks and Country Club. Don's family belonged to the Moose and ate barbecue and hamburgers at the Big Four.[2] Nita and Pete were stay-at-homes in their big house.

Lowney told him about growing up at the jail in Marshall, where her father was sheriff. She told him about being born in Kentucky. She told him her father was in the state legislature and was a Democrat.

"I've been known to shoot Republicans and even Democrats who act like one," she laughed. She knew that Republicans and Democrats took turns running county offices in a friendly way. She told Don how she had picked up a pistol loaded with blanks and shot the state's attorney in the stomach. "He almost died. But you see I did not know that, even though there are no bullets in the gun, the explosions from the powder can be lethal at close range."

Don's grandmother Miller had told him that story with great glee several years before. He now realized that he had indeed heard of Lowney before but had not identified his hostess as the central figure in the Robinson fable.

Don did not tell her during this visit about his family situation, nor about his friendship with Nita (the widow of the couple who had wanted to adopt him when his father first left the family), who lived in a large house with white columns. Don's family owned a modest house. Don was finding his relationship with Nita to be suffocating and demanding, keeping him from socializing with his high school friends.

A man came into the kitchen from an adjoining part of the house, poured a mug of hobo coffee, and joined Lowney and Don at the round table. His name was Jim Jones.

Don was not prepared to meet anyone other than Lowney Handy. He and Jim shook hands and studied each other obliquely while looking at and listening to Lowney.

"Jim is writing a novel that will change the Army," Lowney explained. "And the Army needs changing."

"If I survive it, the writing of it. And Lowney and Harry survive living with me while I'm spilling my goddam guts all over the goddam place."

Don did not think he had heard of Jim Jones before, but later, when he told the story of the meeting to his mother and to Nita, they explained that he was the son of the dentist Dr. Ray Jones. Everyone in Robinson knew about Dr. Jones's suicide in his laboratory and about his being found by his daughter, Mary Ann. Jim was away in the army. Don then remembered Jim from a time when Jim had entered the office while Don was in the dentist's chair. Don was five years old and had hidden under the bed in an attempt to avoid the appointment with the villain dentist.

"I don't like you," he told Dr. Jones.

"I don't like you, either," Dr. Jones said matter-of-factly. "So let's get this over with."

About that time a light-haired boy with round metal-framed glasses appeared and said, "Dad, I need some money. My bike has a flat."

That was thirteen-year-old Jimmy Jones.

Jim's father and Don's father had exchanged services in those days—dry cleaning for dental torture.

Once this memory came back to Don, he also remembered that a man who roomed at his grandmother Miller's had gone on drinking bouts with Dr. Jones not long before he shot himself.

"In three years Jim's books will be as well known as Hemingway's or Wolfe's," Lowney announced.

"God, I hope it doesn't take that long," Jim said with a grimace. "For your sake. And for Harry's. And for Perkins and Scribner's."

Lowney told Jim that Don wanted to be a writer. They wanted to know what he was writing. He confessed that he wrote editorials for the school newspaper and compositions for English classes.

They wanted to know what authors he liked. What had he read recently? What poetry did he like? What was being taught in school? Don felt he was being tested for something he was not even sure he wanted to be a part of. He did read books now and then, but with school and drama rehearsals and going to movies, there was not a big place in his life for books. There was no library in his house or in Nita's house. His aunt Helen had a small collection of books from the Book of the Month Club, and he sometimes read one of them.

"*For Whom the Bell Tolls,*" Don offered. Lowney had just mentioned Hemingway. The novel had been a Book of the Month Club selection and was in his aunt Helen's small collection.

Lowney cocked her head thoughtfully, and with a caress of the words, smiled: "And therefore never send to know for whom the bell tolls; It tolls for thee." Those words from John Donne were delivered with a soft meeting of her eyes with Don's.

For Don this was the first of many quotes to come over the next weeks and months and years, and, although he might have heard the lines many times before, they never failed to affect him when delivered with that final meeting of the eyes. Lowney was a mesmerist.

Had he read Hemingway's *The Sun Also Rises?* Lowney asked him. He shook his head.

"In many ways his best," Lowney said. "Or *A Farewell to Arms?*" He shook his head again. "Hemingway's very good at showing and not telling. That is the secret so the reader has the pleasure of figuring it out for himself," she told him.

Lowney then moved into the next room and invited Jim and Don to follow. It was a bedroom-study for Jim that Lowney and Harry had recently built onto the house. It had a fireplace and stained-glass windows, a large oak desk and typewriter, with light coming through a glass brick window that took up one whole wall. It had its own bath, and it opened out onto a real patio. There were shelves and shelves of books.

Lowney went to a shelf and pulled out two books. "You must read them," she told Don, and placed *The Sun Also Rises* and *A Farewell to Arms* in his hands.

Lowney then asked Don how he liked Jim's study. They were all sitting— Jim in the chair, Lowney on an ottoman, and Don on the couch that made into a bed. She explained that Jim had used some of his army pension money, and some of his advance from Scribner's, and Harry had mortgaged the house for the rest of the money to build the new room.

Those details were not lingered over. They asked if he had read Thomas Wolfe's *Look Homeward, Angel.* Don again had to say, "No."

Lowney, a believer in signs and portents, told Don that Wolfe had been haunted by a number all his life, and when the train brought his body back to Asheville, North Carolina, that was the number on the car that carried his body.

"Have you read Scott Fitzgerald's *Tender Is the Night* or *The Great Gatsby?*"

"No."

All these writers wasted too much of their talent in alcohol and grandstanding, Lowney told Don. She did not intend for Jim to fall into that trap.

Jim had just finished writing a book called *They Shall Inherit the Laughter*, she told Don. But Scribner's and Perkins had turned the novel down. It was all about Robinson, and if he would like to read it they would tell him whom the characters were drawn from. The next book he was writing was about the army, and Perkins had advanced him five hundred dollars on just the outline, because he knew from *Laughter* that Jim could write. The words had almost fallen over each other in Lowney's haste to tell the story.

"What a wonderful room to write in," Don said, wishing it were his own.

"Come see the rest of the house and where I'm working and sweating my own book. It's a murder mystery," Lowney said, leading the way out of Jim's room and through the kitchen to the living room. Don thought the antique chairs and sofas looked uncomfortable. There was a fireplace, with a china clock and candlesticks. The candlesticks were pictured on her bookplate, with her name "Lowney Turner Handy" below them. Lowney was always giving him books to read, and he came to know her bookplate well.

They went up a narrow stairway to "my bedroom," she told Don. "Cherry" she said about the bed. The wood chests were cherry, too. Don had not known furniture could be made from cherry trees. The walls in the room were slanted, and there was a dormer window, but the room seemed dark to him. They went through to Lowney's study, a smaller room. An oak desk, with a typewriter on it, almost filled the room. Above the desk was a framed motto:

REMAIN QUIET AND BE THOUGHT A FOOL.
WRITE A BOOK AND REMOVE ALL DOUBT.

Don liked the way she was showing him the house; she was treating him like an adult.

They went back downstairs, through the living room, through a small room with a music box that played "Take Me Out to the Ball Game." Then they went to Harry's room; it was light and full of windows and bookcases behind a king-sized bed, the first Don had ever seen.

Don and Lowney went back to Jim's room where Jim was listening to music—was it Cab Calloway?—and eating a ham sandwich. The three listened to a few more records, and the questioning began again. Don was to discover in years to come that Lowney, Harry, and Jim would sit down and listen to records but never to the radio and radio music. Don believes the three of them gave their entire attention to the music when they listened to records.

Don reported that he played the piano but not well enough to perform in public. He and friends had hitchhiked to Chicago and St. Louis, though, to hear Stan Kenton, Tommy Dorsey, and Benny Goodman.

Finally, Don decided it was his time to ask a question: "Have you read *The Razor's Edge* by Somerset Maugham?"

"Not his best book," Jim said. "Too sentimental."

Lowney looked knowing but was quiet.

"The main character still haunts me," Don responded, delighted to hit on an author Jim and Lowney had read.

Don turned to Lowney: "Could it be possible that Maugham based his characters on real people?"

Lowney jumped from her seat on the ottoman and pulled two books from a shelf. She said, excitedly, words almost colliding in haste, "Maugham based *The Razor's Edge* on the life of Paul Brunton."

"Did Brunton write books?" Don asked.

Lowney turned to a bookcase: "Here are two of his books: *The Search in Secret India* and *Search in Secret Egypt*."

Overwhelmed, Don could only say, "May I read them?"

The two books by Brunton joined the pile of other books he was taking home.

The whole afternoon had gone by, and it was too late for him to stop by to see Nita as he had planned to do.

Before Don left for California, he introduced some of his high school friends to Lowney and Jim, and while he was away for several weeks they went to her house for sessions of talk about music, philosophy, and life. Lowney had such a bad reputation in some circles in Robinson that his friends went there without telling their parents, fearing they would be forbidden to visit. Don was not aware of Lowney's reputation until Nita confronted him with stories and gossip.

When Don returned his friends were ecstatic, for Lowney treated them like adults and was willing to talk about any subject. She was completely unlike their staid parents or their remote teachers in school.

After he graduated, Don went to work at a local hardware store, clerking until it was time to go to college that fall. He and his friends went to see Lowney as often as possible. Harry—handsome, aristocratic looking, a little remote—was sometimes there. He used a cigarette holder, and the more he drank the more he looked like Franklin D. Roosevelt. Parsimonious with his speech, he often gave unexpected compliments. Jim was sometimes around, too, but preoccupied. It was Lowney they went to see, Lowney who smiled and flattered them. They enjoyed rebelling against the town gossips who talked about her moral failings. They read *They Shall Inherit the Laughter*, which Jim had put aside to work on *Eternity*; they read Lowney's book; they read the bugle scene in *Eternity*.

Don and Lowney were on the patio outside Jim's room on June 29, 1947, when Jim opened a letter from Burroughs Mitchell, a young editor at Scribner's, telling of Perkins's death on June 17. Perkins had championed Jim, writing him frequently, for he recognized the potential of the novel-in-progress.

Before he was taken to the hospital, Perkins had instructed his daughter to remove the two manuscripts by his bed — one of them was Alan Paton's *Cry, the Beloved Country*, the other was a part of *From Here to Eternity* — and make certain they were placed in safe hands at Scribner's. Don remembers the anguish in Jim's voice as he announced that Perkins had died. Lowney was anguished also. She came over to Jim and looked at the letter as he read it. Not only were they distressed by the death, they were also afraid that *From Here to Eternity* might not be published.

In the confusion at Scribner's following Max Perkins's death, it was two weeks before Burroughs Mitchell wrote Jim. Without meeting him, Jim decided that Mitchell would be his new editor, and they had a long working relationship. The news of Perkins's death was devastating to Jim, but he was certainly under better control of his life than he had been when he first came to live with Lowney and Harry. He wrote Mitchell on June 30, 1947: "There was a time not so long ago that I would have gone off on a bat someplace and sweat it out but now I think I will go back to work tomorrow" (*To Reach Eternity* 100).

Lowney and Jim's fears that Scribner's would not continue to support Jim as Perkins had were unfounded, for Mitchell, himself a veteran, effectively guided the long and controversial novel to publication. Mitchell's letters to Jim were soothing, and Jim continued to make progress on his novel.

Don became something of a favorite of Lowney's, and on weekends when Harry was gone on a trip to stay with his girlfriend out of town, Don was allowed to use his desk and room to write. He was trying to write about his impending breakup with Nita. After Pete's death, Nita and her mother had come to depend upon Don as the man about the house. He was seen as the dependable one they could lean on in their advancing years. Don began to chafe at his obligations to make regular appearances at Nita's house, to take her to the movies, or to take her for Sunday dinner and a drive in the country.

Lowney offered Don excitement and intellectual talk and quiet times listening to music — symphonies and jazz. Lowney, Jim, and Don went to movies and then talked about them. Once at a park Lowney and Jim danced together, awkwardly. It was a good summer for all of them. Don, though, faced a major problem. Nita was fighting to keep him, to protect him from Lowney. She issued an ultimatum: Don had to choose between Lowney and Nita.

Don's grandmother Sackrider heard gossip about Lowney when she went to the beauty parlor to get her hair done. Soon more people heard the gossip, and a letter-writing war erupted between Lowney and Nita during the summer of 1947. In response to a letter from Nita calling Lowney a corrupter of the youth of Robinson, Lowney replied: "You can start right now and get your dozens of names of people who will gladly sign a statement that they do not want their sons to come to my house (home). And while you are getting them kindly have them state why and give proof, for you are going to get a chance to use all you can get." Lowney signed her letter "Lowney Handy" under these words: "A woman is a fool who will write me the kind of letter you wrote to me." The letterhead, though, was Mrs. Harry Handy, 202 West Mulberry, Robinson, Illinois. When it was useful, Lowney wanted it made clear her husband was one of the most important members of the community (Sackrider narrative).

In response to another letter of Nita's, Lowney wrote: "It has come to my attention that you have been spreading scandalous filth connected with my name and a young boy who is a protégé of yours. . . . The boy does not concern me, except as I see great promise in his future, and thought you had done a fine piece of working in helping with his training. But if I learn of any more nasty insinuations I shall be forced to go into court and let you have the chance to prove your lies" (Sackrider narrative).

For Don this controversy, which erupted in the summer and continued into the fall after he had gone to college, made him feel like a character in a play, acting the part of a misunderstood young man. Nita had given him an ultimatum: he had to stop seeing Lowney. After much emotional soul-searching he chose Lowney.

Many years later Don thought that Nita and Lowney could have been friends. They both loved antiques. They both liked to have young people around them. Jealousy, though, kept them apart. At the time of the controversy, Don thinks he, Lowney, and Jim all seemed to be enjoying the soap opera. Don might have persuaded Nita that Lowney and Jim were important to him and that they all could be friends, but he did not do so. When Nita issued her ultimatum he used it as an excuse to get away from a smothering surrogate mother, not knowing yet that Lowney's influence over him would also have its problems.

Jim went to New York in the middle of November 1947 to meet with Burroughs Mitchell and other editors at Scribner's and was completely reassured about their support of his novel. He had long conversations with Mitchell and John Hall Wheelock, the distinguished poet-editor. In a long and detailed letter of November 16, he told Lowney about a conversation with Wheelock:

> I told him about how I thought that every real artist's work was really a striving toward discipline, like you and I talked about. I also told him about the Yoga breathing exercises I had fooled with; he asked me if I had trouble sleeping when I was working, and I told him how I put myself to sleep with rhythmic breathing but did not explain the process. Also told him about how I kept a glass of water on the desk, after learning how the Yogis kept a vessel of water by them. He was very interested in this and asked if it increased my energy. I did not go into great de-

tail, but intend the next time I talk to him to explain about Prana. (*To Reach Eternity* 109)

When Don and his friends came home for Thanksgiving, they learned from Lowney that Jim's trip to New York was a great success and that he was due to return soon. Harry drove over to Terre Haute to get Jim at the train station. Don and his friends gathered in Jim's room to get the full story; they and Lowney were all eagerly awaiting the full account of Jim's adventures. When Jim and Harry arrived, Jim was ready to talk, but one of Don's friends kept demanding center stage to tell college stories. Don realized how insensitive the friend was, pulled Lowney into the kitchen, and apologized for his behavior.

"You're so mature to see this," Lowney said.

Don and Lowney went back into Jim's room, and Don told his friend that they had to go, that Jim was tired, and that Lowney, Harry, and Jim needed some time to talk. The next morning Don's friends were at his mother's house for breakfast, and Jim came by and talked to them, saying he and Lowney had decided that, with all the controversy over their coming to her house against their parents' wishes, Lowney did not want them to come there again. Don had been the only one willing to stand up and make a decision when he was handed an ultimatum, and he would always be welcome.

Don's action in clearing Jim's study of the inconsiderately loquacious guest had clearly impressed Lowney. She told Don it was time for him to get serious about writing, to leave school, and to go with her and Jim to Florida for the winter. Don says his mother, Polly, was not too keen about letting him go to Florida with Lowney: "At the time Polly did not make any comments to me. But she told me in later years that she had gone to Lowney and told her she was not concerned about the gossip, but at the same time if she ever did anything to harm me that Lowney would have to deal with Polly" (Sackrider narrative).

At Indiana State Don had been talking to a friend, Charlie Dawes Myers, about writing and the Handys and Jim Jones. Dawes decided he wanted to go along. When Don told Lowney about it, she invited Dawes to come down and meet them. Her decision was that if Dawes could pay his own way (Harry was already supporting Lowney, Jim, and Don there), he could come along. There was a stipulation: there were to be no long-haired "arteests" in the group. Don and Dawes went to the barbershop for crew cuts. Jim already wore his hair short. The Handy Colony had begun in 1943 when Lowney took Jim in. Now it was being expanded. Fifty years after these events of 1947 Don mused:

> I will never really know what went through Lowney's mind in inviting
> me to go to Florida. I still think that in some ways it was her way of giv-
> ing Jim competition. I think Lowney and Jim really did appreciate my

loyalty to them, especially at a time when things were against them in Robinson. I never returned to college, though Lowney did try to get me to enter Stanford.

I was so excited about going to Florida with them I could not keep any food down for several days. If I had it to do over, I would not. But then life with Lowney Handy was an education you could not buy. And I was one of the chosen few. (Sackrider narrative)

Did Lowney choose him by flipping a coin? She often made decisions this way, as Don was soon to learn. Should we take the day off and unwind? Flip the coin. Should Jim give Don the book? Flip the coin. And one could not go back on the coin or ask for two out of three. This became part of Don's education: he made decisions by flipping a coin.

Lowney had been thinking about a formal school or a colony for writers for some time. She had a plan, and she would not be stopped.

White Hall, the Kentucky mansion belonging to Cassius M. Clay, where Lowney Turner Handy was born. Photo by George Hendrick.

Jim Jones in his room at the Handys' house in Robinson. Courtesy of the Handy Colony Collection, Archives/Special Collections, University of Illinois at Springfield.

Lowney and Jim on a trip to Mesa Verde, Colorado, in October 1949. Courtesy Don Sackrider.

Harry Handy sitting on a diving board at the colony. Courtesy of the Handy Colony Collection, Archives/Special Collections, University of Illinois at Springfield.

From left to right: Jim Jones, Don Sackrider, and Willard Lindsay on the way to Mesa Verde, Colorado, in October 1949. Photo by Lowney Handy. Courtesy Don Sackrider.

A group of colonists having a meal at a picnic table. Mary Ann Jones is in the foreground, Jim is in the middle on the left. Courtesy of the Handy Colony Collection, Archives/Special Collections, University of Illinois at Springfield.

Don on the colony grounds. Courtesy of the Handy Colony Collection, Archives/
Special Collections, University of Illinois at Springfield.

Helen and Tinks Howe. Courtesy Helen Howe.

The ramada on the colony grounds, circa 1952. The building contained the kitchen, dining room, recreation room, library, and carport. Courtesy of the Handy Colony Collection, Archives/Special Collections, University of Illinois at Springfield.

DEAR HARRY:

Today Jim received a check for $1000 here, he had wired Mitch,
(COPY OF TELEGRAM ENCLOSED) this is part of money from British
Publisher.   Their down payment was $1500 and the book is to be
published in late fall of 1951 in England, and will bring good
royalties - of course this all means some time before the money comes
in. However, now we are set with a good house, better than Naples.
S tove is honery but rest is really fine, have gas heat -- and room.
Can sleep ten without too much effort if need be and the boys
really like it.   S tove is only complaint, it is a L & H Electric
model(first one made I think) and has had the bottom unit burned
out during war and not replaced, probably out of market by now - so
I try to bake with the top, broiler unit only - and it is a small
apartment size. Of course I can go out to the trailer, which is parked
now behind the house.
We look onto the ocean and I can lie in bed and watch the waves. We
can do that from threeother rooms too. You'll really like it here
and there will be other things for you to do.
Jim has letter from Flair magazine wan ting to photograph him and
run a profile article on him(feature article) for the February issue
to conside with the publication of Book -- LOOKS LIKE A BIG YEAR AND
PLENTY OF PUBLICITY.
We are truly lucky over the house - it was cold the last few days
frost promised even as far down as Lake O - and snow they say in the
Carolinas, so we had a chance to test the house, it is warming up
today and the boys are out fishing. But it's really nice,- large
livingroom - long - has a nook at one end with D on's bed and writing
table.   Sunroom right out toward beach with twin beds for Willy
and Bob and Willy w rites in there. Mary Ann has bedroom (Bob writes
there during the day) and Mary Ann writ4s in diningroom - which is right
off a nice little kitchen. Snug and my bedroom is off diningroom,
which sets it apart with a stool and bowl in it. The bathroom is
off livingroom and MaryAnn's bedroom - small hall there.
It is all parnelled in wood, I think cypress, and stained some, makes
me think of the house my grandmother had when Iwas small.
And always you can hear the sea. And watch it. You'll really like it
I know. The atmosphere is like very young Miami Beach.
People are especially nice and with the publicity(we had to t ake
second spot to Myrna Loy) we are getting the breaks. This is the
best deal we've ever had.   And now rent is paid to March first -
Jim can manage until after your vacation on groceries - so that
will give you a breather.
H e said to tell you he'd write you a long letter in a couple of
days - he's been tired after the trailer hawl down, had generator trouble
several times, or the cable came loose once. I had a smooth
running car all the way down. You tell Art I sure was pleased with
what he did.   We'll have to get him some oranges and take them
back when you come down.
Hope your teeth are alright - and they don't hurt. I ve got one that
I think he should have worked on - but it may just be edgy - am
watching my gum where it has receeded -- but will get by o.k. throught
the year.   We have a laundry right across the street thatw ashes
and ri4s a tubfull for 65¢ -- ;ots of things like that and it
rests me to think of it.
We will be going to work in a few days - just t ook a little time off -
more later and all my love, take care of yourself and don't get
too tired before December- it's just a month away -

A letter from Lowney to Harry, November 6, 1950. Courtesy of the Handy Colony
Collection, Archives/Special Collections, University of Illinois at Springfield.

Grover Ashby, called "Arkie" by his friends, who was the model for Bama in *Some Came Running*. Courtesy Helen Howe.

Jeff Jones, Jim's brother (wearing boxing gloves), on the colony grounds, circa 1952. The trailer behind him was the one Jim used while touring the country. The tents served to house some colonists before the two barracks buildings were constructed. Courtesy of the Handy Colony Collection, Archives/Special Collections, University of Illinois at Springfield.

Lowney and Jim, standing behind his house in Marshall. Courtesy of the Handy Colony Collection, Archives/Special Collections, University of Illinois at Springfield.

Jon Shirota, the last student at the Handy Colony. Courtesy Jon Shirota.

Jim and Gloria Jones, about 1959. Courtesy of the Harry Ransom Humanities
Research Center, The University of Texas at Austin.

4

Planning for the Colony Compound and Completing *From Here to Eternity*

Lowney had a way with new recruits for her writing school: she listened to them, loaned them books to read, made them know she cared about them, and made them feel that, through her, they could become famous writers. With Don Sackrider, Jamie (as Lowney usually called him) Jones, and a few others, she brought them into her personal world as she captured and subdued them. That December 1947 just before the trip to Florida, Lowney and Don sat in the front seat of her car for a private conversation; Lowney explained that they were going to be living at close quarters and she owed it to him to be honest about her relationship with Jim and Harry: She and Jim were lovers, she had to sleep with him to keep him in line to write; she and Harry had not slept together since he gave her gonorrhea, and she had to have a hysterectomy; Harry had his own girlfriend, but she and Harry had made their peace and were friends. She also indicated that Jim would eventually become more aware of difference in their ages, would want a family and leave her. She was prepared for this eventuality. Don was not shocked. He had suspected that Lowney and Jim were lovers but respected their privacy. He was to keep the secret and not speak about it until it became common knowledge.

Don was now securely caught in Lowney's trap. He had been told the "truth" about the Lowney-Jim-Harry relationship and was now part of

Lowney's intimate world. He saw to what lengths Lowney was going to nurture the genius writer in Jim. Don felt she would do the same for him.

Harry drove Lowney's 1946 Plymouth down to Florida. Lowney sat beside him in the front seat and Jim and Don were in back. Charlie Dawes Myers was to fly down a few days later. Don was in a fog of happiness, but he did notice that Jim was tense. Lowney was catering to Harry, who was happy to be out of his office, pleased to be away from the problems at the refinery. After the first day of driving, they stopped for the night, and Harry and Lowney shared a room. Don and Jim were in another room, and Jim complained that it was all show for Harry's ego and, "If that son of a bitch touches her I'll kill him." While Jim was jealous and afraid that Lowney would have sex with Harry, it is also reasonable to speculate that Jim over a long period of time had come to feel guilt about his treatment of Harry, the older man he genuinely liked. In *Go to the Widow-Maker*, Grant (Jones's barely disguised autobiographic character) felt "guilt as an ungrateful son" and "guilt as a man who kept on repeatedly cuckolding his friend" (60).

What were Lowney's motives in making these sleeping arrangements? Harry was financing the Florida stay and deserved to have some of his emotional needs attended to. Although their marriage was unconventional, Lowney sincerely loved Harry, who always supported her. By his presence, too, he was adding respectability to the venture. Away from Robinson Lowney needed to blend in with the conventional members of Florida society. Lowney had also learned to control Jim by making him jealous.

The next day they reached Venice, Florida. They checked into the Kopper Kettle Inn, a large Spanish-style house in a residential area, managed by two elderly ladies. Harry's presence for a few days made it appear that Jim and Lowney were staying together as son and mother in the small apartment at the back of the property. Charlie Dawes Myers and Don had separate rooms in the main building. After New Year's Day, Harry returned to Robinson.

Venice was then a small town with fewer than three thousand people. The boom of the 1920s had gone bust, and there were streets with their old lampposts disappearing into acres of palmetto and pine, streets waiting for houses to be built. In the winter of 1947–1948, Venice was not a prime spot for visitors. It was the winter home for the Kentucky Military Institute and not much else.

Don, Dawes, and Jim worked every morning from daylight until noon. For Don and Dawes, Lowney used a central tenet of her program: copying. She started them with Dashiell Hammett's "A Man Called Slade," as Jim reported, "in order for them to conquer the circumlocution that most beginners have" (*To Reach Eternity* 123). Then she had them type out "Snows of Kilimanjaro" by Hemingway; a story from Nancy Hale's *Between the Dark and the Daylight*; "That Will Be Fine" by Faulkner; "The Ears of Johnny Bear" by Steinbeck; "Life in the Day of a Writer" by Tess Slesinger; twenty pages of

Thomas Wolfe's *Face of a Nation*, with the two students picking which passages they copied; sections from Rebecca West's *The Harsh Voice* and Fitzgerald's *Tender Is the Night*. Later she had them copy more Hemingway, especially a section from *To Have and Have Not* and "The Short Happy Life of Francis Macomber." (Lowney approved of the way Hemingway wrote dialogue and she admired his descriptive talents, but she disliked his macho image.) Jim explained the rationale: "The principle was to not let them copy too much of any one author at a time, so as to be influenced by his style. . . . The point was for each to copy toward his weaknesses. For instance, if one loved poetry she put him to copying the tersest stuff she could find, like Cain, Raymond Chandler, William Irish. If he was a Hemingway addict, she put him to Tom Wolfe or Chesterton's 'Lepanto'" (*To Reach Eternity* 123–24).

The method does have its advantages: typing out a text makes the copyist read the text carefully. The copying makes the copyist aware of the style of Hemingway or Faulkner or Chesterton. There were problems, though. Lowney was not interested in (in fact was opposed to) homosexual writers such as Proust and warned her students not to read him. She was not interested in the theory of writing and warned her students against theoretical works. She discouraged Don, Dawes, and Jim from talking about their work, making them more isolated from the give-and-take of the workshop method used in most college courses on creative writing. In Lowney's method, the students talked about their work with Lowney.

Dawes and Don would copy for about two hours and then turn to their own writing. Dawes was a veteran, five years or so older than Don, and had more experiences to draw upon. Don tried to write about his break with Nita and his meeting with Lowney and Jim, but he was too close to his material to shape it. He was at a formative period in his life, and Lowney gave him another of her central ideas. She bought him a copy of Webster's Collegiate Dictionary and wrote on the inside of the cover: "Shakespeare: 'Fool, Look into thy heart and write.'" Then on the flyleaf she wrote: "To Don from Lowney. Kopper Kettle Inn. January 1948. 'If man is to remain free as God intended him to be he must strive always to be alone in his heart.'"

Jim and Lowney gave Don a hard time. They kept telling him he talked too much and that he needed to be quiet and look inside himself. He was reading widely in the approved texts and admired Hemingway's short stories and Fitzgerald's *Tender Is the Night* because he liked the shallow characters and wanted them to grow up. He wanted to be mature and wished there was a pill he could take or a deep trip into meditation that would allow him to return all wise and with deep insight allowing him to write about life and pass his knowledge on to his readers.

Don's comments on meditation indicate that Lowney was initiating him into occult ideas, as she had Jim. She loaned him a copy of *Concentration and Meditation*, a compilation of teachings by the Buddhist Society of London; she gave him Annie Besant's *Initiation (The Perfecting of Man)*. She underlined one passage in Besant's book: "Our duty is to learn in order to help, and you can only reach the hearts of men by sympathy when you can speak from their standpoint instead of standing obstinately on your own. That is the great mark of one who is truly tolerant, that he can see a thing from the standpoint of another, and speak from that standpoint in order to help." Don gave the occult a lot of credence then—but now comments that the quote "sounds a little like Dale Carnegie's *How to Win Friends and Influence People*."

Jim gave Don the short version of *Light on the Path*, which he inscribed, "To Don—given with my best regards—at point of gun." That and the other books of this nature came from Samuel Weiser's Occult Books in New York. Don was expected to take these works seriously, to work and look within himself, and to meditate and contribute his share of silence.

As the four settled into their routine, Lowney seemed unhappy. The apartment she shared with Jim was small: living room, bedroom, and kitchen. Jim used the living room for working and sleeping, Lowney the bedroom. Perhaps some of her unhappiness stemmed from the domestic role she assumed that winter. She did all the cooking; the writers were not allowed to help, for Don, Dawes, and Jim were to save their creative energy for their fiction. Lowney gained weight those months in Florida and spent much of her time alone in her room.

The meals she prepared were simple—later she pared meals down even more at the colony. Breakfast in Florida was fresh squeezed orange juice, coffee, oatmeal, and toast. Lunch was salads and a casserole or stew with vegetables, and frequently a dessert. Once she made a chocolate pie and put lemon extract in it by mistake instead of vanilla. The three men laughed and held their stomachs as they ate it, but Lowney was not amused. Another time she made a pumpkin pie and did not stir the filling well. Don thought the custard bottom with the pumpkin on top a great idea and asked how she did it. Lowney told him not to be sarcastic.

Even though Don felt repressed at times by both Lowney and Jim, he felt as if he was living the American dream. The old house from the 1920s was stucco with tile work. There were palm trees, and the beach was five minutes away. It was a quiet place with few other guests. An older man with a phonograph with good fidelity would invite the four of them to listen to classical music.

Lowney, in a good mood, would take Don along on an excursion to buy oranges by the bushel from a roadside stand. They then stored them in the shade under the house, and it was his job to go through them and look for rotting ones that might in turn spoil the rest. In such instances, and in the afternoon excursions, Don saw Lowney at her best, not as a carping teacher.

Jim was working well that winter, but he too shared some activities with Don. A few mornings before sunrise the two would drive along shell and sand roads through palms and pines to a dairy to buy milk for breakfast. Don, weaned from Illinois by sun and surf, liked Florida and liked the idea of being a writer and having a house of his own there some day.

After the writing and copying was over for the day, Lowney arranged activities for the three men under her care. They chopped wood for the fireplace in the main house, a room opened for all the guests for reading or visiting or enjoying the fire on cool winter nights. The four were popular with the owners for supplying firewood, and Lowney demonstrated to the men that she was the champion wood splitter.

They went to the beach most afternoons for sunning, swimming, occasionally finding large petrified shark teeth in the sand, and playing touch football. Jim had perfected some of his athletic skills during his time in Hawaii, but Don had never thrown a football until that winter. His playing with kids his own age had been interrupted by the divorce of his parents.

After their five hours of concentrated work, Lowney might take all of them to Sarasota to shop for groceries or to go to the movies. Lowney had Don read about Edgar Cayce, the psychic, and soon took her charges to a local fortune-teller. Jim was told he would have great success as a writer. Don was told he would have success, but the numbers fifty-one and fifty-two came up, and the fortune-teller did not know if those were the years or the age. Nothing startling happened to Don in 1951 or 1952, and he turned fifty-one and fifty-two without incident. Lowney was a true believer in the occult and no doubt could have later spun out a story of the significance of the numbers fifty-one and fifty-two. She certainly agreed about the predictions of Jim's coming success.

Lowney also took them to see the mansion of John Ringling in Sarasota. In a large gallery of baroque art they saw the collection of Peter Paul Rubens's work. Lowney lectured about the nudes, how it was the fashion to have them plump. In those days before *Playboy*, Don had never seen such female nudity, but Dawes and Jim, older veterans, must have had different reactions from Don's. Lowney's interest in exposing her students to art, architecture, and beautiful interior furnishings was something she put aside when the colony in Marshall was underway, for then she concentrated on an enclosed environment for her students, who brought their experiences and their aesthetics with them. She might have acted differently had there been cultural opportunities in Marshall, but there were virtually none.

At the John Ringling mansion Don witnessed Lowney at work selling Jim, the author of the next great American novel. She was like her father, who garnered votes to become county sheriff or state legislator whenever and wherever opportunity arose. She spread word about Jim to visitors at the mansion that day, and having two other writers with her made her even more credible as a teacher. Lowney used the same technique for selling Jim and his forthcoming book whenever she went into bookstores. She carried in her purse copies of letters from Maxwell Perkins and Burroughs Mitchell that praised drafts of chapters of *From Here to Eternity* and showed these to the manager and clerks in the store. If Jim were with her, she would introduce him all around. Wherever Lowney went she was selling *Eternity*.

Still, most afternoons were spent in physical activities. If Jim's work was going well and Lowney was late in announcing lunch, Don and Charlie would read at the pool. If Jim finished early, before lunch the three men would take an hour to relax by practicing archery or knife throwing at a target.

Lowney's favorite pastime, other than writing and nurturing young writers, was shelling. She exposed her three charges to the beauty and variety of shells, and they all became hunters for cat's paws and cat's eye shells. The most exciting finds, however, were sharks' teeth, some enormous, some small, many in razor-sharp perfection, all reminders of violence, death, and destruction.

As pleasant as sunning and game playing and shelling and moviegoing and cultural activities were, Don was under pressure, as later colonists were also to be. At least once a week Lowney would come to his room for a private meeting. She would tell him he must look inside himself, that he should not be afraid to bare his soul, that he should work, work, work, as Jim did. The reason Perkins had given an advance for *Eternity*, she would say, was that he knew Jim could and would work. She would tell Don to take advantage of this time in Florida, because few people found the time from school or work or family to write. When she left with a soft smile there would be a tear in at least one of her eyes and in both of his. Or was it the other way around? Lowney did not shed crocodile tears, but she was an actress, and she played set pieces for her writers.

Dawes was more mature than Don. He was paying his own way that winter, and Lowney and Jim treated him gently. He did his writing, and Lowney conferred privately with him. Since Jim, Dawes, and Don were not supposed to talk about their writing or about other writers, Don was unaware of Dawes's subject matter and of his progress.

Lowney, though, was not reluctant to talk about the work of her star pupil. Don and Dawes knew that Jim's work was going well and that he had a good working relationship with Burroughs Mitchell, his new editor at Scribner's. They also knew that he had sold a story, "The Temper of Steel," to the *Atlantic Monthly*. Jim had sent five stories to Edward Weeks, editor of that journal, in September 1947. He suggested he was a good candidate for an "Atlantic First," awarded to writers who had never published before. He bravely insisted, "I'm going to be one of the best to come out of the New Post War Generation, or whatever they will call it" (MacShane 95).

Weeks sent proofs to Jim in Venice, and Jim and Lowney could now believe that his long apprenticeship was ending. Jim wrote Mitchell on January 20, 1948, about this subtle story: "Lon, you see, is really a killer, a man who kills with no compunction whatever and not the dilettante hanging around cocktail parties. . . . I meant to show Lon as the result of the tremendous advance in indoctrination since the last war, a member of Hemingway's generation" (*To Reach Eternity* 120). He hoped that Weeks chose the story because he understood the concealed point. When he collected the story in *The Ice-Cream Headache*, Jones added a note to make his meaning clear: "The point is in the reference to Archie Binns and the quote about chivalry being dead, and in the boy's comparison of his own cold-blooded killing of the Japanese to the comparable scene in *All Quiet*. This is what modern warfare has come to be, with all of our blessings, and God help us for it" (11).

As a way of celebrating the acceptance of the story, Lowney, Jim, Don, and Charlie went to the local drugstore fountain and had three ice cream sundaes each—one strawberry, one chocolate, and one butterscotch.

Don's mother called him in March to report that Nita's mother had died and that Nita needed him since she was now alone. Nita's mother had been good to Don. She had not said anything when he had broken with Nita months before. He had known her all his life. She had taught him piano and corrected his grammar and pronunciation. Her insistence on speaking proper English was well ingrained, and even though he was in a fog of bliss just to be with Lowney and Jim, he found it difficult to get used to their barracks room talk. Don, though, admired Harry's speech with its Franklin Delano Roosevelt overtones.

Don's mother seldom interfered with any of his decisions, but this time she kept saying, "Nita needs you now," and urged him to return for the funeral. Finally, Don said, "I'll let you know."

Lowney was intent in participating in the lives of those close to her. She, Jim, and Don conferred around the table in the small kitchen.

"Writers have to be SOBs. There will be something all your life to take you away from your typewriter," Lowney told him. "It is difficult to be both a nice guy and a writer. Look at Gauguin. He left his wife and child to paint. And Jim's brother Jeff wants to write. I told him his time will come when he finishes raising his kids. It's like if you want to run off with your best friend's husband and leave your kids, you can't expect everyone to approve. You can't have it both ways."

"She's right," Jim said, "you can't be both a gentleman and a successful writer." Jim was echoing what Wheelock had told him the previous November: "Wheelock remarked . . . that Samuel Johnson wrote that no man could be both a writer and a gentleman" (*To Reach Eternity* 107).

Don could not decide what to do. The conference went on for an hour. Nita had cared for him since he was nine months old. He did not want to be obligated to her again, but he found it difficult to ignore his mother's repeated line: "She needs you now."

Finally they all agreed that Don should sleep on it before he made a final decision. Why did he decide to return to Robinson? Don can now speculate:

"Maybe it is simply the way men go off to war because they need a change. Maybe I was already tired of the copying and looking into myself."

At breakfast the next day, after Don announced his decision, it was agreed that if he left there was no coming back to join them that winter. Don knew this might mean the end of his attempt to become a writer.

Don was in Robinson to attend the funeral, but later in the day when he went to the house to express his sympathy Nita snubbed him completely. Don was now in limbo. He wanted to write, but he could not return to Florida. He had no money and stayed with his aunt.

Lowney and Jim returned in time for her birthday on April 16 that spring, and Harry, following a long-standing policy of employing students, gave Don a summer job at the refinery mowing the lawn. So Don had enough money to take a room, and he wrote in his spare time. Lowney decided that he should enter Stanford in the fall and be on his own. It was typical of Lowney to plan the future of those around her, even someone who had temporarily strayed from her by returning to Robinson for a funeral. It was that summer that Willard Lindsay came into the group.

Willie Lindsay had graduated from Robinson High School in 1946 and had been a student at Indiana University before he came into Lowney's orbit in the summer of 1948. He was good-looking, rather like the young Cary Grant, with a sly and bawdy sense of humor, and southern speech patterns. His father had died after the financial crash of 1929, but the family still had money, certainly more than Don's.

He was joined that summer in visits to Lowney's house by Tinks Howe and Russ Meskimen. Tinks had been a childhood friend of Jim's throughout their schooling in Robinson, had served in the army, and had returned to Robinson at loose ends. He was soon visiting Lowney and Jim, his longtime friend. He was good-looking and robust, with an infectious sense of humor. Unlike Jim, he was not in psychological distress when he returned from the army. He had an active mind and was a careful observer of events around him. His mother, a nurse, was one of the few women in Robinson who did not judge Lowney's attitude and behavior harshly, and the two women were friends. Tinks, too, was nonjudgmental and sympathetic to Jim, Lowney, Harry, and those on the fringes of Robinson society. He did not, however, have a drive to become a writer as Jim, Don, Dawes, and Willie had.

The other visitor to Lowney that summer was Russ Meskimen, used as the basis for the character Dave Hirsh in *Some Came Running*. He was older than Jim and had a romantic past. He had left Robinson under a cloud before the beginning of World War II and had gone to Hollywood where he wrote for the movies. Or was it for soap operas? Upon his return to Robinson he was one of those lost people who looked to Lowney for help, who seemed to need her authoritarian ways. Whatever the truth of his writing career in Hollywood, he expressed a desire to become rich and famous with Lowney's help.

Don decided to follow Lowney's plan for him and enroll at Stanford. He could not enter until the spring semester but went out to Palo Alto to arrange for work and a place to stay. Still, he was distressed not to be in Florida with Lowney and her pupils the winter of 1948–1949 but he and Lowney often corresponded. He went to Madison, Indiana, for a time, living on his savings while he tried to write. Lowney did not invite him to go to Florida that winter. He went to New Orleans and joined Dawes who was working on his writing there. Don found a job, and the two played at being artists in the French Quarter.

During the summer and fall of 1948 Jim continued working on his novel. Perkins and then Mitchell kept encouraging him to go on with *Eternity*. Lowney went over his work with him, but she seems not to have been deeply immersed in the problems of the aspiring writers she was welcoming. Once his writing for the day was over he could play games or have a beer with them, but he did not become psychologically entangled with them as Lowney almost always did.

Early that fall of 1948 Lowney started preparing for the usual trip to Florida, but this time she planned to take a larger group: Tinks Howe, Willie Lindsay, Russ Meskimen, and Jim Jones. There were immediate problems. Russ was enamored of Katie, a local woman, and did not want to abandon her. Lowney was enraged, for he "spouted a lot of Yogi" at her. To her mind it was "Twisted Yogi. Yoga means union and not with one person and certainly [not] one for sexual reasons." Lowney believed that writers and would-be writers had to keep away from marital entanglements. Jim apparently knew of Russ's planned defection, and Lowney wrote that she "called [J]im on being to[o] cowardly" to face her. She was in a towering rage; she called Russ's girlfriend a whore. She wrote Russ that if he didn't come to Florida he had to repay Harry the $130 he had borrowed. It was an emotional time. She wrote Harry that she had "to speak true. It makes things rock and you get in on the bounce but I must do it. Although I'm always planning on being a person who never gets angered." Angrily she scrawled on the typed letter: "He never intended to go" (undated [fall 1948], UIS).

Russ's hesitation about joining Lowney's group was just the first of many problems. Willie's mother was outraged that her son, from a good family, was consorting with such a dubious person as Lowney. She wrote her son:

> Has it ever dawned upon you Willard that you have allowed a woman who has never been a mother to influence you?
> Do you realize that she took you to Florida—you were just twenty—not twenty one and that I could have made it plenty hard for her. Law is law, you know.
> Because *you are you*, a boy who has had a nice home life and love and advantages, the whole town is in an uproar—some of the other followers had nothing to lose.

> Don't misunderstand me—if you want to write all power to you. But
> you are not doing a thing down there that you could not do at home
> and be in wholesome surroundings and at the same time have a job with
> lovely people.
>
> Shelby Harrison was shocked to hear you had gone. As you know
> he too is interested in writing and works at it a couple of hours a day
> but he realizes it might never amount to anything and one must be
> practical. . . .
>
> If you had had a father Mrs. Handy would *never never* have done what
> she has done to influence a boy of sterling principles such as you have
> always had. Everybody thinks so. (October 9, 1948, UIS)

Lowney sent the letter to Harry in Robinson, with a wry comment about his
keeping her out of jail for violating the Mann act by taking a minor across
state lines. She went on:

> Willy [both "Willie" and "Willy" are used to refer to Willard] is writ-
> ing his mother diplomatic letters—conceived by myself—and we should
> be able to handle her from this end. Of course she can't do anything.
> And it doesn't bother me what people do—but I know it is often em-
> barrassing for you. Sorry. But I guess it just has to be. When you come
> out ahead they'll have to be convinced. But how people hate to have
> me accomplish anything by going out of the old system. Willy is really
> going to hit. He shows much much more promise than Don or Dawes
> did. You'll be surprise[d] when you see his work.

Lowney seemed to realize how volatile the situation was. She wrote of all of
them with her in Florida "sitting on a nice bed of coals," and she wondered
if the good citizens of Robinson had "tried to get at you more than half a
dozen ways" (October 12, 1948, UIS).

After a few weeks Tinks Howe, not burning to be a writer, left the group.
He had a unique gift for friendship and maintained his ties with Lowney and
Jim. Russ was another defector. As the winter progressed, Lowney was almost
out of control, nearing a breakdown. Jim returned to Robinson, returned to
his own room in the Handy house, returned to the quiet of a house shared
with the patrician Harry, who was certainly not given to emotional outbursts
as Lowney was. Harry was never a father figure for Jim. He was generous and
remote and regarded Jim as Lowney's project: she would rehabilitate Jim and
make him into a famous writer.

Lowney was working on her own novel, *But Answer Came There None*,
and was taking sedatives. Some of her letters from this period reflect her
hyperactivity, others the state of depression induced by her medication. At
times she railed against Harry's mistress and spoke of divorcing him and eventually marrying Jones, though she would give Jim time to be a celebrity first.
These threats and promises were not to be, for it was Harry who supported

Lowney and her writing ventures. Moreover, their bonds were too strong to break.

Even though Jim was far away from her, she still subjected him to her own brand of sexual and psychological warfare. Jim had told his brother: "I had to be *broken*. . . . Lowney cut the ground out from under me until I had absolutely no place to stand. I was completely lost. Every way I turned for aid or escape, Lowney was there to cut me off" (MacShane 88).

In January 1949 she wrote to Jim suggesting that one of her brothers in Marshall could find a girl for Jim to satisfy his sexual needs. (It appears that Lowney was becoming more reluctant to sleep with Jim, and she even spoke of her frigidity in other letters of this period.) Jim responded that he would not allow her brother to be a procurer. He was going to win Lowney back. They were both romantic, he wrote her, but she had turned to the asceticism of yoga while he continued to yearn for "Love of a woman, a mate, a comrade, an equal, a meeting in body, a meeting in mind, a meeting in spirit" (*To Reach Eternity* 125).

Jim wrote her on January 27, 1949, that when he had first met her, Harry was the dominant partner: "He even had you convinced you were just about to go crazy" (*To Reach Eternity,* 129). Earlier in her marriage, he thought, Lowney had been dominant. The supremacy battle was starting again, this time between Lowney and Jim, she using yoga and asceticism, he using sex. Later explaining her use of the Hindu system, she wrote Jim:

> You feel that my Yoga is something I've used against you. It wasn't a conscious use. I ached for something that I could see that led to something. In the life I was living—in nothing at all could I see any promise until I developed my faith. I had to have something more than you or myself as individuals to believe in—and I had to have some explanation of why I had suffered all my life. . . . Perhaps my great faith in your writing came out of Yoga—but you have more and more chosen to put your own lack and failure on this mystical something that you couldn't or wouldn't attempt to understand. (undated, UIS)

The arguments in the letters are nonlinear. All the old problems and all the new problems between the two lovers spill out in the letters during the late winter of 1948–1949. Jim said that Harry wanted Jim "to go out and sleep with something, anything." He told Lowney she talked about her pupils too much, and then he declared, "I have never been your pupil" (*To Reach Eternity* 131). Jim then segued into thoughts on writing a love novel in the future: "It will end as a tragedy, of course. But yours and mine must not end that way. It has been too great a thing, for both of us. It has made both of us, though it nearly destroyed us both a thousand times." In his emotional, logic-defying letter, Jim argued that he did not "want sex anymore, but I do want it occasionally with you. If I have to go without for months at a time while we are apart working until we can get enough money to set everything up right so we can be close but still free to work, then I'm willing to do that. I'll go without not only because it destroys you for me to do it, but because I don't want it otherwise" (132).

In her letters Lowney often wrote that her own fiction was not going well. She kept trying, feeling that if she could make a sale of her work she would be more confident. She clearly felt that a writing teacher should be able to publish her work, but she was never able to do so. She was a compelling storyteller, but she could never turn her oral tales into coherent fiction.

This was a time when Jim wanted a Jeep and a trailer to pull behind it, vehicles for the open road and escape. In the midst of her confused letter, scrawled pencil notations in the margins, she made a plea: "Also let's see if we can't become a committee of two to help Harry to get some fun into his life — it must be horrible — such heavy work. . . . He's more than earned it with us. You stop being stand-offish because you think he's trying to get me away from you. . . . I do feel that you don't take your debts with Harry very seriously. If you are to grow up you must meet him as a man and not as a child who expects to be humored and given whatever he cries for" (February 3, 1949, UIS).

To Lowney Jim was still a child, and she claimed a perfect right to tell him how to act. At the same time she was urging him to act like an adult, she was writing him the kind of letter a high-strung adolescent might compose. There were too many ideas, too many bruised egos, too many old grievances for expression in this series of letters. Even as he tried to win Lowney back, as he lamented that she could not read his manuscript daily and talk it through with him, Jim announced he had never been her pupil. He was declaring his independence even as he was insisting that he loved her and needed her.

The arguments that circled throughout these letters turned on the central question of sex. With his strong sex drive, Jim was forced to deal with Lowney's growing asceticism, her withdrawing of her sexual favors. He would write her, during this crisis, of their abandonment to sexual pleasures during the early days of their affair and his present perplexity about how to win her back. The issue of sexual versus platonic love was one he attempted to cope with. Lowney kept insisting that Jim used sex to dominate her, that when he wrote her about a stray meeting with a girl in Robinson that could have resulted in sex but did not, this was a way of controlling her. Part of her rage was that her protégé was not as submissive nor as dominated as she wanted him to be. The issues were partially resolved with Jim declaring his love for her, Lowney declaring her love for him, his sending chapters from book 4 of *Eternity* to her for her editorial comments, and finally his admitting: "Of course, you'll have to help with every other book I write, too. I will need you with me to begin something else. It just looks like I'm always going to need you, and theres no way we can get out of it, I guess, is there?" (*To Reach Eternity* 139).

That crisis weathered—though Jim's acceptance of Lowney's views on sex does not seem convincing—he wrote her, "You're right that we need to get a light on sex. I'm beginning to think its only our different definitions of it" (*To Reach Eternity* 139)—the lovers were more harmonious for a time. Harry purchased the jeep and trailer for Jim, which helped, for Jim could roam more than before. At times Lowney would accompany him, but at other times his companion was Willie Lindsay.

Living in trailer camps was cheap. Jim liked the sociability and the blue-collar people he met in the ramadas and laundry rooms of the parks. He had socialized with working people in Robinson—with the town gambler and Russ, the ne'er-do-well, and with some of Tinks's friends.

In a trailer camp in Memphis, he met workmen at a local bar after he had finished his work for the day. Nearing completion of *Eternity*, he was to write about such people in *Some Came Running*. He said they were "a stiff, proud, independent bunch" and that "if you admire crafts and skills you can't help but like them" (MacShane 94).

Lowney joined Jim and Willie for a time in Memphis but soon returned to Robinson. She was not in good health and was given to using self-treatments: faddish diets, enemas, megadoses of iron capsules. At other times she took sedatives prescribed by a doctor. She wrote Jim the end of May 1949 that she was thinking of checking into Barnes Hospital in St. Louis. Jim responded that her health problems were probably caused by frustration and nervous strain, but that a checkup was called for (*To Reach Eternity* 147). Lowney made no secret of her problems. In the spring of 1949, Lowney told Don that she was having emotional problems and that Jim was going to take her away on the road.

Late in the summer of 1949, Jim, Lowney, and Willie left for New Mexico, Colorado, and California. *Eternity* was almost finished, and Lowney was readying her own novel for submission to Scribner's. *But Answer Came There None* was a mystery. Burroughs Mitchell had to tell her that the "design seems helter-skelter" and that the reader did not care about the characters in the novel. Lowney sent a transcript of the letter to Harry with a letter in which she admitted, "A story should flow naturally out of what the characters do. I had so much Yoga and ideas that I wanted to get into the book that my story didn't flow. I preach" (February 3, 1950, UIS). Lowney could guide and edit and inspire writers, but she herself was not usually a disciplined writer.

Jim was under great pressure as he neared the end of the novel, and he welcomed Don, who flew out to Albuquerque to be with the threesome in early fall. Willie and Jim had bought Western hats and tight-fitting Levis, and Don did not even recognize them at the airport. Don had joined the army, hoping the discipline would help him organize his life. He had just completed basic training. The four of them were in high spirits and made an excursion to Mesa Verde in the southwestern part of Colorado to see the Indian cliff dwellings. The clear air and the starry skies at night as they sat around a campfire at Mesa Verde were clearly restful for Jim, who needed a break from his writing. Lowney seemed to be in control of herself and in charge of the trip.

One day while Don was in Albuquerque with his friends, they all went over a story he had written called "To Spite Your Own Face," about an intellectual and the problems he faced in basic training. Mostly, though, the four just had fun, in spite of their poverty. Harry sent what he could. Tinks, who had been given a job at the refinery by Harry, also sent much-needed money. The vacation over, Don returned to army service, hitchhiking to Washington, D.C., for he was as broke as Jim and Lowney. The others moved westward.

Willie's story "A Busy Day" was published in the *Ladies Home Journal* in September, another validation for Lowney and her method of teaching. She was a star maker. Don now believes, "I don't think the fact that Willie's brother-in-law's brother was editor of that magazine had anything to do with it being accepted there, but it might have got the story in the door and read."

On October 30, 1949, still in Albuquerque, Jim sent Burroughs Mitchell the chapter on Pearl Harbor. He made major claims for it: "I . . . believe it will stack up with Stendhal's Waterloo or Tolstoy's Austerlitz. That was what I was aiming at, and wanted it to do, and I think it does it. If you dont think it does, send it back and I'll re-write it. Good isnt enough, not for me, anyway; good is only middling fair. We must remember people will be reading this book a couple hundred years after I'm dead" (*To Reach Eternity* 151). Lowney was in complete agreement. She had, from the very first, believed Jim would be a major American writer. Harry had supported Jim with funds and had helped give him some stability, but Lowney was the midwife who had presided over the birth of the novel.

The threesome moved on to Tucson, where it was warmer than Albuquerque. Jim was working on the chapter in which Prewitt is killed. Jim wrote Harry on November 18, 1949: "I kind of hate to do it in a way. I've got so used to the son of a bitch being around. But my first loyalty goes to the book" (*To Reach Eternity* 152). Jim spoke of their poverty in the letter. Harry had sent some money, and just in time: "I think we had about seven cents, all told. That noon, before it came, we . . . needed a quart of milk and a loaf of bread so we compromised and bought the bread and used canned milk in the gravy."

Harry joined the group for an excursion into Mexico, but that trip was not satisfactory because of the primitive conditions they found there. Harry returned home, and the other three moved on to a trailer park in North Hollywood, California. Jim was working feverishly on the novel, but there was also time for socializing. They visited Don's mother, who had moved west, and

Willie's aunt in Pasadena. On the grounds of the trailer park, they met a writer whose novel would be made into a movie featuring Lucille Ball and Desi Arnaz under the title "The Long Long Trailer." *Eternity* was completed on February 27, 1950. Jim wrote Mitchell he was on his third martini. He defended the last scene between Karen and Warden—the love scene without sex. He told Mitch, "I think you'll agree with me it couldnt have been any other way" (*To Reach Eternity* 154). That scene is obviously a dramatization of the love-without-sex emotional conflict between Lowney and Jim during the late winter of 1949. Lowney was probably happier with that scene than Mitchell, who did not know about the passionate statements in the series of letters between Jim and Lowney.

Jim was in a magnanimous mood in his letter to Mitchell. He acknowledged that others had made major contributions to the novel and he was planning to write a proper acknowledgment. He did so, thanking Maxwell Perkins, John Hall Wheelock, and Burroughs Mitchell. Then he thanked "Mr. and Mrs. Harry E. Handy of Robinson, Illinois, without whose initial impetus I would never have started out to be a writer at all, and whose material and spiritual expenses over a period of seven years provided me with necessary nourishment." He was correct: without the efforts of all those people *Eternity* would never have been written.

In the letter to Mitchell, Jim went on to praise Lowney's novel, which Mitchell had rejected. He declared that it had "a lot of fine possibilities" and that "the sad thing, the funny thing, the really ironical thing, is that she has put so much time [in] on me, and on Willy, and Don, and several others who have not panned out as well as either of these, that she has neglected herself. I intend to see that she does not go on doing it. The truth is, I'm excited about the damn thing. Her book" (155). Lowney's book was never published, however. She was caught up in the excitement of the publication of *Eternity*, the plans for the colony, and Jim's next novel, *Some Came Running*.

This was a turning point for Lowney, for she had to decide to give up friends, reputation, and her own writing in order to become a full-time teacher of writers. Tinks Howe has said that Lowney worked for years on a book called *From Riches to Bitches*, "about the social circle in Robinson," a manuscript she apparently burned on a beach in Florida. Tinks believes Jones adapted some of that material in *Some Came Running* (Lennon 208–10). At later times, Lowney would talk about continuing to write, but she spent most of her creative energies teaching. Nevertheless, her fiction—and her talk about her fiction—had a considerable influence on Jim, beginning with *Laughter*.

When Don chose Lowney and Jim and Harry over Nita, Lowney told him the story of a seeker who was searching for the "Initiation," and the guru said, "The path to the right is smooth and easy and full of comfortable inns along the way. The one to the left is hard and rocky and there will be many storms along the way. But Ah! Look at the blue sky in the distance."

Lowney came to a turning point when she started plans to transform the informal Handy Group into the Handy Colony for young writers. She had been dreaming about finding a primitive, isolated spot where aspiring writers would be housed and fed and she would direct their work. It was destined, she believed, that *From Here to Eternity* would be a success and that writers would want to study with her, undergoing her successful but unorthodox methods. She believed she could begin and implement such an audacious plan as early as the summer of 1950. Lowney believed she and the writers around her would help people and society by discussing social problems in their fiction. She was far from being a systematic thinker about social issues, but she did impress on her students the need to investigate them.

The correspondence of late 1949 and early 1950 indicates that her emotional problems had lessened. The trip west had helped. Her Jamie's getting near the end of the writing of his novel also helped. Her plans for a writing colony compound certainly helped. Harry offered his complete support of her plans.

Jim had reason to feel elated and very tired that February 27, 1950. The long years of work on the composition of *Eternity* were at an end, and his editors at Scribner's recognized his achievement. Mitchell was filled with praise; John Hall Wheelock had written him, "without romanticizing anything, there are moments when from reality itself, presented with fidelity, an exalted kind of poetry is wrung." Lowney wrote Mitchell (Jim surely saw the letter): "I have given seven years of my life, one track mind, fight, praise, my family and my friends, my own writing included, in order to have a hand in the creating of a *great* book" (MacShane 97–98). Jim had agreed to give her 10 percent of the royalties from the novel. The publicity surrounding *Eternity* brought Lowney and her plans for the colony to public attention. The royalties from the novel and Harry's continued financial help made it possible for her to establish and support her writing school.

5

The Colony Gets Under Way
in Marshall, Illinois

Before *Eternity* was finished, Lowney had told Jim that she wanted to share the fame and adulation she knew was coming to him. Once the novel was finished, she was ready, also, to work behind the scenes to control the publicity, for she knew that she and her lover had much to hide. First, though, the manuscript had to be edited and printed.

Jim stayed on in California for a time, but Lowney in this quiet interlude returned to Robinson. Within a month after *Eternity* was completed, Jim began to face the problem of censorship. He wrote Burroughs Mitchell on March 18, 1950: "One of the things I would like you to remember is that the things we change in this book for propriety's sake will, in five years, or ten years, come in someone else's book anyway. . . . Writing has to keep evolving into deeper honesty, like everything else, and you cannot stand on past precedent or theory, and still evolve" (*To Reach Eternity* 158–59).[1] He went on to assert that *Eternity* was not salacious.

Mitchell and Horace Manges, attorney for Scribner's, found words and passages in the manuscript they felt should be deleted if the book were to be saved from Comstockery. Jim was of divided mind about the proposed expurgations. He thought the editors at Scribner's were being too cautious. After all, the setting was the American army in Hawaii just before and after Pearl Harbor. To omit or severely restrict the use of such words as *fuck, cunt, snatch, pussy*, or *piece of ass* would reduce the realism of the life Jones was attempting to capture. There were also important scenes marked for omission. The description of a wet dream had been excised. Jim protested: "I want that to stay in. I saw that, with my own eyes and—with very little variation—I saw it a great many times. If it is illegal as written, then maybe I can cut it inside, a word or two here and there, to make it a little more palatable, but I want it in. Christ, Mitch, the people of this country dont know what the hell goes on in it. Maybe thats why they're such sanctimonious bastards" (*To Reach Eternity* 163). Jim could not save that small scene. He was not able to retain most of a scene in chapter 9 where Warden and the clerk are talking about painters. He wanted it in because it showed "a particular depth of character in Warden that I want" (161).

Over forty years after the editing of *Eternity*, the reader's sympathy is certainly with Jones when he told Mitchell: "You think I put those things in arbitrarily, just for simple shock value. But it isnt that. You see, you were an officer. Officers are inclined to be a little more polite about such things." He went on to argue, "us American men of the lower classes" were interested in "cunt," not love. He objected to Mitchell's suggestion to substitute the word *pinups* for *cunts* (162).

In the meantime, Lowney was in Robinson and Marshall planning the first session of the colony she had long dreamed of founding. Relying on the generosity of Harry and his mother, she began her artistic haven in Marshall that summer of 1950. Marshall was a small rural town north of Robinson. It is the county seat, but it did not have the industrial foundation that helped to support Robinson. Harry Handy's mother, Mrs Handy, lived in a large Victorian house that faced the east-west Cumberland Road, also known as the National Road (now U.S. route 40), and behind her house, quite isolated, was a five-acre cow pasture. It was here that the colony was to be built. Jones returned to Illinois from California and began to refer to this venture as the "Marshall Plan." U.S. dollars flowed to devastated Europe in the plan bearing General Marshall's name; Jones's royalty checks from *Eternity* would flow in to help keep the colony going. In the summer of 1950, though, Jim was poor, and Harry was the colony's financial angel.

Jim, in his letters, gave a clear picture of the beginning weeks of the colony. Behind Mrs Handy Senior's two-story house was a "deep, pretty steep natural draw heavily grown with brush and willows," and on the other side of that draw was the cow pasture. To get water and electricity to the colony, Jim and Bob Smith, a former student at the University of New Mexico who had joined the colony, dug a "2½ ft ditch from an outside faucet over at the house clear down one hill across the half-swamp in the bottom and up the other hill." The wiring for electricity was complicated, and Harry sent "boys from the plant" to do that work (*To Reach Eternity* 168). Harry routinely sent materials and laborers at the refinery up to the colony. He even filched a refinery building and had it moved over to the cow pasture. Lowney's brother Harold was in the plumbing business and provided help.

Soon a cabin was moved to the grounds and remodeled for Lowney, who was still living in Robinson and driving up to Marshall, about twenty-eight miles north of Robinson, three or four times a week. Later, another cabin, more elaborate than the first, was put up for Lowney. Her second residence was at the front gate of the colony, which was reached not from the Cumberland Road but from a small side street. This second cabin was remodeled and enlarged. Don Sackrider remembers that "Lowney loved to make something from nothing—as she had their house in Robinson: It had been a three room shotgun house which became a special comfortable mixture of new and old with impeccable woodwork and paint. Slim (the refinery carpenter) was mostly responsible for the built-in bookshelves and kitchen cabinets in the Marshall cabin. Lowney loved fireplaces and had one added to that cabin immediately. There was a sleeping porch (screened) added on off the small bedroom" (Sackrider narrative). The cabin did not look like much on the outside—David Ray said that the paint was peeling—but the interior was comfortable. Lowney's first cabin became Harry's when he was there and was also used by overnight visitors to the colony. Harry, with his quiet dignity, was a source of peace and harmony when he was on the grounds of the colony. She depended on him more than most people knew, and she could even joke that Harry had to become an alcoholic in order to live with her. With affection, she told the colonists that one Sunday morning Harry, suffering from a hangover, mistakenly put on the shoes of her young brother Harold and walked downtown for the newspaper. The shoes pinched his feet all the way, and Harry kept saying to himself, "I've got to quit drinking" (Sackrider narrative). Lowney had humanized Harry for the colonists. They could approach him after one of Lowney's outbursts, and he would work behind the scenes to seek solutions to their problems.

That first summer, Jones wrote in his letters, facilities included Lowney's original cabin, two trailers, and one tent with a brick floor. Bob Smith was in the tent. Jim occupied one trailer. Alma Rae Isley Akers and her twin daughters, aged twelve, were in the other trailer. Lowney came to dislike working with women; in her opinion they were defensive, resisted criticism, and were egotistical. She may have taken Akers in because she was said to be a first cousin of Jennifer Jones, the actress; because their fathers owned a chain of movie theaters, and because Jennifer had influence enough to get Akers a screen test. Lowney may have been a rebel, but she stood in awe of celebrities and of the rich and powerful. Several forces were at work in her personality, including a degree of insecurity at odds with her forceful personality.

Over time two barracks buildings with five cubicles each, a ramada, a laundry room, showers, and toilet facilities were added by the contractor John Snedeker. "Harry's boys" (borrowed from the refinery) were at times called on for plumbing, electrical, and carpentry work, with the colonists driving a lot of the nails.

The summer of 1950 set the pattern for years to come at the colony. The Akers twins were copying fairy tales. Alma Rae Akers was copying Hemingway. Bob Smith was typing out "Hindu Yoga and Hammett and Raymond Chandler." Don Sackrider was getting out of the army and was joining the Handy gang. "Behind it all," Jim rightly acknowledged, "is the guiding-light, whip-cracker, and guardian-angel . . . Lowney" (*To Reach Eternity* 170).

The colonists copied and did their own work during the morning and worked on the grounds in the afternoon. Harry sent up used bricks, and patios and walkways were put in place. It was undoubtedly a good thing that Jim had all that physical work to do, for the publisher's demands for changes in the manuscript were growing, and he needed relief from these mounting problems.

Jim went to New York at the end of the summer for conferences with Mitchell and Manges, going over the fifty galleys Manges thought might cause trouble. A love scene between Prew and Lorene had to be drastically cut. The "Unguentine" section on the relief provided by sex was omitted. Some parts of the scene with the homosexuals were changed. References to "one-way, two-way, and three-way girls" were cut. Jim set to work revising and recasting some scenes, for he wanted to be published and sincerely wanted to avoid legal problems (*To Reach Eternity* 173).

Jim's account of the editing had comic overtones, in spite of the damage being done to the manuscript: "Manges had a 'score sheet' he had kept while reading, and there were 259 fucks, 92 shits, and 5 pricks. He did not count the pisses for some reason. Well, Mitch and I went through later, working in the Scribner office and cut the fucks [to] 146, the shits to 45." Jim returned to Marshall before the negotiations were over. Manges approved of the rewrites in the text but still wanted more omissions: only 25 or 26 *fucks*. Mitch disagreed, for he had promised "to print the fucks in unprecedented scale" (*To Reach Eternity* 173–74). Mitch and Manges had cut the *fucks* down to around 106. Back in Illinois, Jim gathered friends and neighbors, as if for a corn husking, to go over the manuscript to make final deletions and enter the changes demanded by Manges.

With all the demanded changes, Manges felt he could defend *From Here to Eternity* in New York, but he was unsure about Massachusetts. Mitchell's reaction: "to hell with Mass" (174). Jim tried to be philosophical about the mutilations of his manuscript, but his true feelings are to be found in his remarks and pleas such as these in the margins of many pages of the manuscript: "This is needed. Cut for obscenity only" and "I sure hate to lose this." He had written a much better novel than he was allowed to publish. He gave the manuscript to Lowney, with the understanding that it was to be returned to him after her death. All of his later efforts to recover the *Eternity* manuscript were foiled, however, and it is now in the Rare Book and Special Collections Library of the University of Illinois at Urbana-Champaign.

The negotiations over the expurgation of *Eternity* went on for a long time, and it was Jim, largely without the help or interference of Lowney, who did all the negotiating with Mitchell and Manges. Lowney was busy with the colony, which stayed in operation until cold weather came. The colony buildings were not winterized, and Lowney, often with her students, went to warmer climes in the winter. Don Sackrider was with the Handy group again. Willie Lindsay spent much of his time at home in Robinson, where the living conditions were more comfortable.

Always looking for distressed souls for she was a healer of the troubled, teaching self-examination and catharsis through writing, Lowney took Jim's sister, Mary Ann Jones, into the colony. After Dr. Jones's death, Mary Ann (who had been the one to discover his body) lived with her brother Jeff for a time before running away to live out on the fringes of society. The youngest of the family, she experimented with drugs, married an abusive African American, attempted suicide, wandered the country with a girlfriend posing as prostitutes. The two young women would take two rooms, bring their two Johns to one of the rooms, but lock them out of the room occupied by the two women. She was in Hollywood for a time, where she tried (and failed) to become an actress. In the past she had stayed many times with Lowney and Jim in Robinson. Now Lowney set her up in a trailer at the colony, to work on an autobiographical novel called *The Third Time You Killed Me* (MacShane 126–27). At the colony Mary Ann was still troubled emotionally and physically, but Lowney and Jim seemed unaware of her deep-seated problems.[1] Don remembers Mary Ann as beautiful in a Debbie Reynolds way. She had trouble with her weight but fasted several times at the colony and frequently had a beautiful figure. She had a clear, true singing voice that Jim was proud of.

The Handy Colony student list for 1950 includes eleven names, but this list is incomplete. Some of the students may have been working with Lowney by correspondence and not actually in residence. Lowney had rules and regulations. Colonists were not to leave the grounds without permission. Liquor was forbidden—but this did not apply to Jim and certainly not to Harry, a confirmed alcoholic. Copying and writing went on from early morning, with copying taking only an hour, except for newcomers who might copy for a somewhat longer time. The colonists worked on the grounds and played at various games. Lights went out early. Breakfast of instant coffee (Don says toast, jelly and jams, and butter were also abundant) was prepared by each colonist. Lowney felt the morning's work could best be done on an empty stomach. Lowney prepared simple casseroles and stews for lunch. She also brought in summer produce and there were salads, corn on the cob, and strawberries. She insisted on using brown rice for health reasons; she also had colonists drinking hot Jello. On special occasions the hand-cranked freezer was brought out for home-made ice cream. At supper time colonists made soup and sandwiches with lunch meat and cheese or peanut butter.

David Ray, a colonist who was very unhappy with Lowney, in "Mrs. Handy's Curious Colony" charged that the colonists were ill fed, but this seems unjustified. There may have been a few of Lowney's faddist notions in the diet she provided, but her avoidance of fried foods and her emphasis on fresh produce was certainly healthier than the usual American diet of 1950. Lowney also had the "faddist" view that smoking was unhealthy. She did not smoke, but Harry and most of the colonists did, and for some reason she provided free cigarettes to colonists, perhaps because most of them had seen military service and were heavy smokers.

There is no doubt about it that Lowney ran the colony along the authoritarian lines of a military unit. Harry until 1951 paid the bills. She was top sergeant. She gave the orders, and she brooked no objections. She had the colonists in, one by one, to go over their progress and their written work. Students were not to talk among themselves about their work-in-progress. She might speak of employing the workshop method, but her two-person workshops were unlike anything used in current creative writing classes. In the best of times, Lowney talked quietly and humorously to colonists, regaling them with stories about her family and things she had seen and done. Scenes of high tension at the colony were actually infrequent, but they did happen and the stories about Lowney on a tear became part of the folklore of colonists' experiences with her.

It was easy enough to accuse her of being anti-intellectual. She often called intellectuals phonies. She wrote (and often said): "I DISLIKE TALKING ANY KIND OF INTELLECTUAL YAK-YAK and find that the people who talk inflate their egos and never work" (Sackrider narrative). She would not allow the colonists to read the works of Marcel Proust, T. S. Eliot, D. H. Lawrence, Dylan Thomas, among others, because she considered them "intellectual and sissy-like" (Wood and Keating xvi–xvii). She must have known that banned books rarely go unread, and it is likely that the colonists read, then or later, the books they were forbidden to touch. Although there were anti-intellectual elements in Lowney, she was also interested in ideas and read widely, though not systematically. She could misread literary works and, as several have pointed out, argue passionately for her misreadings. She was, however, often astute in her judgments, especially concerning writers such as Wolfe, Hemingway, Dos Passos, and Steinbeck. She bought books in large numbers and loaned them to students and friends, and she was often at her best when talking about books and ideas.

Harry was usually on the grounds in late afternoons and on weekends. In addition to overseeing construction projects, he was a stabilizing presence, even though he did not go against Lowney's wishes. Too, if a writer wanted to go home for a weekend and had no funds, Harry would give him money from his own pocket for gasoline or bus fare and meals.

Lowney's brothers and sisters came to the colony often, as did Harry's elderly mother (who felt that Harry had married beneath himself). Lowney always treated Harry's mother with respect, but their relationship was not close. Mrs. Handy enjoyed the happenings at the colony. Lowney always made a fuss over her and told everyone that Mrs. Handy Senior was also working on a novel.

Fall came late that first year of the Handy Colony, and camp was broken on October 31. The sky was blue; the maple trees on the grounds were still brilliant yellows and reds. Bob Smith, Don Sackrider, and several others went down to Florida with Jim and Lowney. Jim was pulling his trailer behind his Jeep. For Don it was a sensuous time. As they drove through Alabama they could smell the harvested peanuts roasting under the warm fall sun.

That fall in Florida, Jim began to give more thought to his Russ Meskimen novel, to appear years later as *Some Came Running*. Lowney was busy planning publicity for Jim, the novel, and herself. As she had done in the past, she visited local bookstores to sell Jim and the forthcoming *From Here to Eternity*. In the meantime Scribner's, long aware that *Eternity* had the potential to be a blockbuster, was preparing a major campaign to publicize Jim and his massive novel.

In this quiet time of his life, soon to change, Jim concentrated on planning his next novel. Like Thomas Wolfe in *Look Homeward, Angel,* he was to draw easily recognized portraits of people in Robinson. His childhood friend Tinks Howe, now working at the refinery, had helped him observe in Robinson the blue-collar underclass and the world of the flamboyant professional gamblers.

One major character in the novel was based loosely on Russ Meskimen (the same Russ Meskimen who had earlier refused to become part of Lowney's writing group because of his love for his girlfriend, Katy). One of Jim's early ideas for the story was suggested to him by Harry, who had been confronted by Katy's husband, an ex-marine looking for his wife when she came back to Russ, her true love. Jim had already decided on another major character, a teacher at the local college in the story (read: colony) and her father, to be modeled on Mr. English, a high school English teacher who had taught Jim (in reality, most of the character traits were Harry's). He would also have "Rebels and Gamblers" in the novel. The gambler Arkie was named Bama in the novel and was to be one of his most inspired characters.

Work on the next novel, though, was soon interrupted. Studios in Hollywood were interested in buying the rights to *Eternity*. Jim wrote Mitchell on December 2, 1950, that he had two requests. First, to get as much money as possible for the sale. He failed to realize what a major work of movie art Columbia Pictures was to make of *Eternity*, for he wrote, "I dont give a damn what they do to the movie; the book will stand by itself after the movie is forgotten." Second, Jim wanted to work on the script, because he wanted "to write a goddam novel on Hollywood. A really good one has never been done, with the possible exception of [F. Scott Fitzgerald's] *Last Tycoon* which was not finished. And, if I make a little money in wages while doing this, I will not complain of that either" (*To Reach Eternity* 178).

The Scribner's sales staff was busy behind the scenes, and the novel was offered to the Book of the Month Club, known for its selections reflecting middle-class values. The editorial board members found *Eternity* "one of the most impressive novels they had read in many years." The club's booklet, however, contained a special statement: "In spite of its unusual quality, we decided to present it to our members as an alternate, instead as a regular selection, for reasons which will be clear to all who read the book. It is not the kind of novel to be put in any reader's hands without warning. Its barrack-room language is unvarnished, and some of the episodes will come as a shock to readers who have led sheltered lives" (cited in *To Reach Eternity* 179). Ten million or so Americans who had served in the armed forces during World War II certainly had not led "sheltered lives" nor had millions of other Americans. Undoubtedly, though, many of the "sheltered" were quite willing to read a book breaking numerous taboos concerning language and subject matter.

J. P. Marquand, the respected novelist then serving on the Book of the Month Club editorial board, wrote Jim a particularly perceptive letter arguing that the *New York Times Book Review* should have given *Eternity* front-page coverage, which gave him much pleasure. Jim at that time was far from sure that the literary establishment would accept him and his novel, and Marquand gave him validation just as Lowney had.

From Here to Eternity was published on February 26, 1951. There was tremendous media attention focused on the writer who had come out of nowhere (it was said) and to his sprawling novel with a cast of characters presented with great skill. Many of the characters — Prewitt, Friday, Warden, Bloom, Maggio — were drawn from life, just as Thomas Wolfe had done in *Look Homeward, Angel*, with only minor changes in their names, personalities, and actions. Others, such as Karen Holmes, were more composite creations. In Karen's case, some of her personality and her troubled marriage with a husband who had infected her with venereal disease and her subsequent hysterectomy came directly from Lowney's history. In addition to the vital sense of the lives of the characters, Jones pictured the peacetime army just at the beginning of World War II as it had never been pictured before.

It is not surprising that most of the reviews were favorable. David Dempsey in the *New York Times Book Review* called *Eternity* "the work of a major new American novelist." He asserted that "in James Jones an original and utterly honest talent has restored American realism to a pre-eminent place in world literature" ("Tough" 2).

The Colony Gets Under Way in Marshall, Illinois

Jim and Lowney at first remained in Florida after the publication of the novel, reading reviews and receiving word from Mitchell about the excitement *Eternity* was causing in the literary world and about the huge sales of the novel. Jim then left for New York to help with publicity, and Lowney corresponded often with her other students. She wrote Don Sackrider on March 15, 1951:

> Don't worry about a thing. LET YOUR EGO die a slow death. If you look inward and think of your story and your book characters that is all. . . . PUT YOUR MIND ON YOUR CHARACTERS. LET THEM DOMINATE YOUR LIFE. Nothing else is half as important. . . . Had letters from two more publishers and had a long distance call this morning from Random House in New York—wants to come see me or visit at Marshall. I told him I had four novels that soon would be ready—he wants to see something now but I said we never sent [a manuscript] in until it was as good as we knew how to make it. NEW YORK IS ALL AGOG AND VERY ENTHUSED OVER ALL OF YOU—they can't figure it out. [One editor told her that he] had never heard of anything like our group in the country. I told both Random and Doubleday something about the books—ages etc. Buil[t] you all up. I told him I didn't know what had happened—it was like a volcano had blown up in a field in Marshall, Illinois. He agreed. Don't worry about yourself. I'VE BEEN TRYING TO GET YOU TO FORGET YOURSELF all these years. Could you divorce yourself from the picture (ego) you have of one Don S. you'd get amazing results. FOOL LOOK IN THY HEART AND WRITE.

Lowney was filled with ideas and plans. The next day she wrote Don: "Both you and Willard work like troupers. You'll be just as much a success as Jones. I promise. And you know I keep them. Also told Random House that I would only work with people who would give my boys all THE BREAKS. I am now in position to write my own ticket—and you can guess how I'll write it. Tell Willy what I've said." Lowney was being courted by publishers and agents who felt that, if she could help develop a talent such as Jim's, she must have other young writers of great potential. Lowney told Don to read the reviews: "Then you can see what is coming up for each of you in turn. . . . You'll be called out on the stage and I'll have to watch every step you make like I am now with Jim—only then I'll have help because Jim is going to do all he can for each one of you" (Sackrider narrative).

Lowney then used praise to build him up, praise based on Emersonian optimism, Hinduism, theosophy, and perhaps *How to Win Friends and Influence People*. "So that leaves it all up to you. YOU CAN MAKE YOURSELF BELIEVE WHAT YOU PLEASE. Your own thoughts are your worst enemies. Nobody can hurt us except those we love or hate. Our thinking again. So concentrate on good thinking. Tell yourself positive day-dreams. BELIEVE." She suggested he copy Willy's story "Busy Day," knowing no doubt that Don—living in

Robinson then, as was Willy—would pass this word on to Lindsay: "Between you and me I think it a much better story than either one Jim published. It's got a flow that hides the technique. It's really good for a youngun." Lowney flattered her protégés when she felt they needed praise, but at times she also deflated them to keep them off balance. Also characteristic of Lowney, she ended her letter by suggesting that Don copy, in its entirety, "*Christian Healing* by Filmore—it makes you think positive." She added in her distinctive scrawl: "Maybe Willy will want to copy it also."

Excited, Lowney was writing Don several times a week. On March 26, she wrote about Jim's interviews in New York and was thinking about the story *Life* was to do. "Did you dream it would come so fast?" she asked rhetorically. "I have known in my bones that it would all along—but I expected it to take several months maybe a year—even five maybe. But we will really be treated. We must have made magical climbs—because the highest test of all is *can you take success*. And because you fall so far if you can't—have you read the Fitzgerald biographies? We must be ready to handle it. I think Jim is—with me always standing behind him cogitating."

Lowney reported to Don that reaction to Jim and his novel was coming in: "In my beauty parlor—I hear by the grapevine that most of the femmes think it a scandalous book and Jamie an ignoramus and illiterate man. Funny thing, you can hardly find a female who has read it through—bet there's not more than ten all told—but you should hear the waves of conversation. I made them all mad and left them to get over it. They may or may not but it never bothers me. I've been trained to withstand that—as you well know." Jim had reported to her that 180,000 had been printed, and Scribner's was contracting for paper for another 50,000 copies.

Lowney was always nervous and agitated when her Jamie was in New York away from her. She allowed him to chase women in Robinson and Marshall, just as she allowed Harry to have a mistress, but on her own turf in Illinois she could monitor Jim's womanizing. When he was in New York, she had little control over him and she imagined (sometimes correctly) that he was drinking far too much and that he was finding women only too eager to spend time with him. As a safety measure, she kept preaching—to Jim, and to all the male colonists—that women would be the death of the artistic life, for women wanted marriage and children and a comfortable life, all of which, she declared, were detrimental to serious writers. Lowney's constant stream of letters to Don indicates just how nervous and agitated she was about Jamie's absence.

Jim's stay in New York was hectic, with interviews and more interviews. Lowney was not a part of the first wave of publicity, but her day was to come, with Whipple's article in *Life*. Not without reason people in Robinson and Marshall who had long gossiped about Lowney and Jim were impressed with the article, "James Jones and His Angel," when it appeared on May 7, 1951. Those in the know, such as Tinks and Helen Howe, thought it ironic that

Lowney had managed to write an article in *Life* but did not get a byline. Even the naysayers in Robinson and Marshall were getting used to Jim's being a star. Many people in those communities who had believed there was a love relationship between Lowney and Jim decided they must have been wrong since it was not even hinted at in the story. Whipple mentions that this was the first article she had permitted about her role in Jim's success, and it is clear from the text that she was managing Whipple and the photographer, just as she managed Jim and the colonists.

Helen Howe, then recently married to Tinks, comments: A shy—retiring—Robinson housewife "wanting no credit or publicity for what she had helped to accomplish—Not Hardly. Lowney thought about teaching others as she had taught Jim from the beginning. She encouraged most of the young people who were around her to see what they could do creatively. I don't remember her ever refusing to accept credit for her influence—with Jim or anyone else. She didn't beat you over the head with it; she just made sure you were aware of how interested she was and the effort she was expending" (Howe narrative). Helen rightly notes that if there was ever a typical Illinois housewife, complete with apron and broom (as Whipple let Lowney present herself), it was not Lowney.

The "mother" image as it comes through in the *Life* article was one that Tinks Howe did not accept, either. He certainly never thought of her as "motherly" where he and other young friends of hers were concerned. He saw her as a friend, interested in his well-being and determined to see that he (and they) did what she thought was best. He considered her role more that of a keeper or warden than of a mother. Don and Tinks also felt that the impression given in the article that Harry was a father figure for Jim was not correct. Perhaps they were seen as father and son because Lowney and Jim were portraying themselves as mother and son to those who did not know the full story. Most of what Harry did for Jim (and he was very generous), he did for Lowney. Tinks said, "Any feelings Harry had for Jim were based on Lowney's happiness."

Helen rightly points out that Lowney cleaned up her image concerning the "four-letter words" in *Eternity*. In the Whipple/Lowney version, Jim thought that even though Lowney was rebellious she might "still be enough of a small-town lady to find this a little too much to take" (Whipple 150). However, Lowney had used this language as long as Jim had known her. Former colonist John Bowers remarks, in his novel *The Colony*, that he was a little giddy when he heard Lowney, an older woman, say "fuck" (20). She used all the four-letter words in her conversations but always avoided being salacious. Once at the colony, Don remembers, Jim warned a colonist not to say anything suggestive or salacious in Lowney's presence (Sackrider narrative). Helen states that "Lowney was the first woman I ever heard talk this way as a matter of course. I once thought she was trying to shock me because

I was then such a naïve person, but I later decided she just talked that way. Certainly she could carry on a conversation and never say a word that wasn't proper, but it didn't happen often" (Howe narrative).

Helen is also amused by the idea expressed in the article that Jim was embarrassed by the attention he was getting and did not want. The first time Helen met Jim after she married Tinks, he was acting the "star" and *Eternity* was not yet even published. "He loved impressing the little people," Helen says, "with his superior knowledge and was usually upset if they knew more about the subject than he did." Lowney would try to keep him from acting out the star role, but he would never stop trying—and succeeding when she was not there (Howe narrative).

The Whipple/Lowney article, which steers completely away from the Lowney/Jim/Harry love triangle and concentrates on Lowney's role as Jim's angel and on her new role as teacher at the colony (complete with photographs of the whole gang), must be seen now as amusing and ironic. But millions read the long, well-illustrated piece, and a significant number of would-be writers immediately decided that Lowney could do for them what she had done for Jim.

Jim had aged in the few years since he left the army, and in the large, full-page *Life* photograph of Lowney and Jim, he looks almost as old as she. In that photograph both are conservatively dressed, though he has loosened his collar and tie.

Helen Howe met Lowney and Harry a week after she married Tinks in June 1950. They met Jim at a tavern, and since it was raining, Jim asked for a ride and invited them to come in so that Helen could meet Lowney. Helen knew Lowney for the rest of Lowney's life, and her comments are reflections of the first impression and the many times she saw Lowney later:

> Lowney was the most confident woman I ever met. I still think she was in a class by herself when it came to who she was, what she wanted, and how to achieve it. She was not a beautiful woman, but she was very attractive, and she made no effort to make herself more attractive. Her hair was frequently in braids; she seldom dressed up; her favorite outfits were jeans, slacks, shorts, dirndl skirts, peasant blouses or halter tops, no shoes or sandals. One day at the bank she stood in line with me. She was barefoot, in a peasant skirt and blouse, pigtails, no makeup. This was at a time when many women went to the bank wearing a hat and white gloves to complete their outfit. She was in complete control of her life and the lives of those around her. The only times I ever saw her not in control were the few times she came to see Tinks's mother when things were bad. (Tinks's mother was a sympathetic listener and had sound judgment. Lowney would discuss with her the best way to handle problems.) I am sure there were very few who saw her like this. She was a very passionate woman never liking something or disliking something a little. It was all or nothing. She didn't appear to hate, but she did dis-

like with a vengeance. She knew the attitude of many people toward her, and she didn't appear to care and only mentioned it to make a point. (Howe narrative)

Helen was aware that most Robinson people thought Lowney weird, perhaps even dangerous, especially where young people around her were concerned. The feeling toward Harry was quite different because, as superintendent of the refinery, he was able to hire and fire. (His aristocratic bearing, however, made many feel he was stuck-up.) He hired Tinks, who stayed at the plant until retirement. He hired Don and many others for temporary jobs. Most people in Robinson, Helen believes, felt sorry for Harry because they thought he did not know what was going on between Jim and Lowney. Helen continues to believe, based on everything she and Tinks knew, that Harry was certainly well aware of their affair and even approved or, at the very least, accepted it. In his fictionalized account, *Go to the Widow-Maker*, Jones makes the same point that Harry accepted the situation.

Helen met Harry the night she met Lowney. She has commented: "Harry was an attractive man with his cigarette holder and his air of control. I remember being amazed at the way he seemed to control his surroundings when I knew Lowney was doing it. He was a very gentle and considerate person who never criticized or offered an opinion when others were being critical. I never saw him angry or being unkind. I never heard Lowney and him argue or have any kind of disagreement. She treated him with the utmost respect and he her."

Helen observed Jim at first hand, and she also could draw on Tinks's recollection, for Jim and Tinks had gone to school together and had known each other for years: "Jim had an ego that was second to none. He loved to play the part of big writer in the making and was always very aware of the impression he was creating. Like Lowney he seemed to delight in shocking people with his dress—jeans, when everyone didn't wear them; boots, when they were not worn by many in Robinson; a battered cowboy hat and a knife in his belt, not usual in Robinson, either. He was more a 'Persona' than a person when others were around. When there were only a few of us, Lowney, Harry, Tinks, Willy, me, he was just like everyone else" (Howe narrative).

A sensitive man, who read widely and perceptively, interested in going to museums and the theater when he was in New York, Jim could also be crude and boorish. Lowney was partially responsible for this part of his act away from Illinois. She had advised him to act the part of an Illinois hayseed when he was on the East coast, for he would be more likely to have his wishes and demands met. To this boorish, hayseed behavior was added, when he was drinking heavily, even more boorishness as well as vulgar language and the threat of violence. He had been stretched almost to breaking point after his return from Guadalcanal; the years with Lowney and yoga calmed him only sporadically.

The novel was at the top of the best-seller list for week after week, and Columbia Pictures paid eighty-two thousand dollars for film rights to *Eternity*. (The Oscar-winning movie version of *Eternity* starring Montgomery Clift, Burt Lancaster, Donna Reed, Deborah Kerr, and Frank Sinatra was a commercial success.) Before it was time for the colony to open in the late spring of 1951, Jim and Lowney were in Hollywood for Jim to work on the film script. They went out to California on the Santa Fe Super Chief, a train often used by movie stars. Lowney later told Don that, on that trip, Marlon Brando saw Jim's huge Indian turquoise bracelet. He came over and grabbed Jim's arm and demanded to know where Jim had bought it. Script writing, though, was not a happy experience for Jim; he did not gather material for a Hollywood novel as Mailer had done; he was soon back in Robinson and Marshall to work on the Russ novel and the colony.

Jim wrote Mitchell on May 31, 1951, that he was excited about getting back to Dave Hirsh, the Russ Meskimen character in *Some Came Running*, because of "his explosive effect upon the town of Parkman, Illinois: thats what really intrigues me. His advent will change damn near everybody's life in the town . . . ; and we'll get a damn good ironic picture of social structure in action" (*To Reach Eternity* 181–82). Jim also reported to Mitchell that the Marshall Plan was moving along. A new cabin was almost finished; Harry had sent Slim to do the interior woodworking, and the plumbing was being put in. Letters from would-be colonists had come rushing in after the *Life* article in May, and Lowney had chosen three new colonists.

Jim was now pouring money into the colony. He wrote Mitchell he needed more money. There was not enough room for all the writers, and they were building a barracks with five small cells, each one just large enough for a bed and a desk. He believed this rather crude building would cost thirty-five hundred dollars. More money was needed for the ramada, screened for comfort, containing an enormous kitchen, tables for meals, and bookshelves for the library, a carport, and a darkroom for Jim. He did not even have an estimate for the cost of the ramada, but it was certainly more costly than the barracks. In 1951 Jim spent between twenty-five and twenty-eight thousand dollars on the colony ("Notes Re Handy Colony," UIS).

Jim also needed money to purchase a large lot just outside the colony gate, where he was to build an elaborate bachelor house. Once Lowney got Jim housebound in Marshall, she could have even greater control over him, though Jim seemed unaware of this at the time. He needed three thousand dollars for a down payment on the lot, and between ten and fifteen thousand dollars in all for expenses, through the end of the year. This estimate proved unrealistic. The ten thousand dollars from Scribner's was almost gone by August 1. The Marshall Plan was expensive in Europe and also in Illinois. Jim also bought a Chrysler for over four thousand dollars, a new trailer, camera equipment, guns, knives, and clothes. He had only four hundred in his checking account and needed more money transferred from his royalty funds. After his years of poverty, low pay in the army, being supported by Harry, Jim spent and spent, and not always wisely. Lowney, too, was not always a careful spender of colony funds. In a letter to Jim, Lowney wrote, "Neither of us can hold on to money or manage" (undated, UIS).

Where did all the money go? In addition to the items listed above, Jim bought gifts for Harry, expensive sports equipment for himself and for the colony, and a state-of-the-art sound system for his Marshall house. He was an avid reader and spent what was needed to build a large personal library.

Lowney rarely bought expensive clothes. Her Robinson house was already furnished with antique furniture. She did, however, acquire books—sometimes fifty at a time. Her money disappeared because of colony expenses (food, typewriters, cigarettes, money for the colonists' sprees in bars and whorehouses) and because of her expensive ways. She was generous to those around her—giving gifts and making loans she knew would never be repaid. Harry was a shrewd businessman, but he did not interfere with the profligate personal spending of Lowney and Jim, probably because he generally let Lowney have whatever she wanted.

That year at the colony, fifteen students were listed as pupils of Lowney's, though some of the fifteen may have worked by correspondence. Mary Ann Jones was there. Willie Lindsay (though he preferred the comfort of a home in Robinson) and Don Sackrider, the Old Boys, were there. Robert Smith was back, as were many attracted by the free publicity in *Life*.

How did Lowney choose which applicants to accept and which to reject? In notes concerning the Handy Colony, Jim wrote that Lowney made the selection and that she usually required the applicants to do six months of correspondence work—reading, copying, and writing on their own. If the correspondence work was satisfactory, then she interviewed the applicant in person. Jim and older members of the colony met the applicant and then expressed their opinion. This account is a rather idealized one. John Bowers gives another version in *The Colony*: Lowney tended to choose the most troubled of those seeking admission. We can also speculate that she saw herself as the self-appointed savior of the downtrodden and as the guru of the aspiring artist.

Lowney was interested in determining whether or not the person could become a good writer. She was concerned with the applicant's sincerity, willingness to work hard, ability to work with her and to fit in with the other colonists. Lowney sometimes asked Jim his opinion about a story or chapter, but this was not often. Lowney was the teacher; she was in control.

Lowney and Jim were famous in the summer of 1951; he was trying to cope with his new position in life and work on his next novel. The newer colonists were in awe of him—and of Lowney's teaching methods, which they felt would make them famous also. Most seem not to have been bothered that Jim made no pretense of living by Lowney's colony rules. He mixed his martinis in his trailer; they were forbidden liquor. He came and went according to his desires, though he conferred with Lowney about his travels; they could leave only with Lowney's permission. He read what he wished to read; they were told what to read.

There was a constant ebb and flow of colonists. New ones were always coming in, and others were leaving, some because they could not take the regimen or because Lowney decided their work was not good enough. Jim realized there were several who just hung on and had to be asked to leave, "writers being like other humans who always like a soft touch if they can get it" ("Notes Re Handy Colony," UIS).

In her dealings with New York editors, Lowney was bravely predicting that "her boys" had four novels nearing completion. She was being overly optimistic. It was several years after *Eternity* before any of the colonists were able to place a novel.

With Jim's money available to her, she was able to expand the colony. Two cabins were in place, the ramada, and a barracks building (another barracks was later added), and there were bricked areas for tents and a swimming pool on the property. The ramada, with a Bedford stone fireplace, a dining area, and shelves for books, was the central meeting place for the colonists.

In the afternoons they helped with the construction, drove nails, and were gofers for the contractor. On the north side of the ramada were terraced concrete steps leading down to the swimming pool. Harry had a bulldozer from the refinery sent in to dam the small creek and enlarge the pool area, which was lined with brick and cement also diverted from the refinery in Robinson. Colonists spent many afternoons removing cement from the used bricks to be were used in the pool and for the walks between the buildings. In general there were no outside visitors except for members of Lowney's large family, Harry's mother, and "important" guests such as Burroughs Mitchell, Norman Mailer, and Montgomery Clift.

Lowney and the colonists were the subject of much gossip in Marshall and Robinson. Some local citizens in Marshall even believed that Lowney had started a nudist camp. Lowney went her own way, probably amused by that charge since nudity was certainly not allowed. The colonists lived in unair-conditioned buildings and were often bare chested, but they invariably wore pants, shorts, or bathing suits.

Jim sometimes mixed freely with the colonists, but at other times he was distant, distracted by his work and by his personal problems. Work on his next novel moved slowly, and he was still gathering information and stories. Through Lowney's brothers, Harold, Andy, and Earl, Jim mixed with some of the local people and helped put aside some of the negative stories about Lowney's folly. Jim was also an active part of the bar scene after the success of *Eternity*. He already knew much about Russ, and through Tinks Howe and others he was brought into the orbit of Arkie Ashby (the "Bama" of *Some Came Running*), a colorful local gambler. Jim was having lengthy and beery conversations with the renegades and castaway men of that part of Illinois and with the factory girls out for a good time. He was sleeping around with the women he met in the bars, but Lowney mostly let him go his own sexual way when he was near home. Her dislike of sex had not changed, and it seems she was glad enough to have Jim fill most of his sexual needs elsewhere, as long as her power over him was not threatened.

Lowney's laissez-faire attitude was different when Jim was in New York, however. Early in 1952 he went to Manhattan to accept the National Book Award. During this trip he met Norman Mailer, William Styron, and other writers, and he saw a great deal of Mailer and Styron during that New York visit. One night when they were in Greenwich Village, Styron put his arms around the shoulders of the other two and said, "Here we are, the three best writers of our generation" (*To Reach Eternity* 183).

Jim's ego expanded during these days, and Lowney grew deeply afraid he was going to escape from her, an inevitable development she herself had predicted to Don Sackrider years before. She suspected he was sleeping with secretaries at Scribner's, that women were throwing themselves at her now famous protégé. She even suspected, or pretended to suspect, that Jim might be infatuated with other men. In an increasingly desperate fight to keep him, she was willing even to make him doubt his own manliness.

Lowney, in Florida, began to make frantic calls, to track him down. He was not in his hotel room, not at the Scribner's offices. Angered and distraught, she was forced to write him, threatening to go into Miami for a binge; no doubt Jim knew this to be an idle threat, since Lowney did not drink. He had been assuring her that he went out with other writers for "light" drinking and talking. Once Jim received Lowney's hysterical letter, he tried and failed to reach her by phone and then wrote her: "I told you before I left that trust and love are what makes people big. You agreed. I hold tight onto my mind that if you did go to Miami for a binge you still wouldnt be able to do it. But if you *did* do it, I still wouldnt care because I love you, and God knows I've done enough to you in my lifetime. . . . But I want you to know: This time I havent." Lowney, in a desperate mood, apparently threatened to leave Florida, to let Jim go from her life. He assured her, however, "It would be a shame, if now you've got the kind of love you want, after paying such a high price for it, that you yourself would destroy it. I hope you wont. I *believe* you wont" (*To Reach Eternity* 183–87).

Lowney did not let Jim go. She entangled him even more. He had bought a plot of land just outside the colony gate and decided to build a bachelor house there—a fine house situated within earshot of Lowney's cabin. In fact, from her windows she had an unobstructed view of his property. Harry planned and supervised the building of the house while Jim and Lowney were in Arizona during the winter of 1952–1953.

The Handy Colony had been incorporated in September 1951, with three people on the board of directors: Jim was the secretary, Harry the treasurer, and Lowney the president. The stated intent was "To develop and further creative writing in the United States, and in connection therewith to operate a home or colony to assist writers and authors, and, in general, to carry on educational activities of a general literary nature" (certificate of incorporation, UIS). Despite storm clouds on the horizon, Lowney, Jim, and Harry believed it was going to succeed.

Lowney turned more of her attention to the colony as Jim worked slowly on his novel. There were inevitable blowups as Lowney dealt with students who sometimes did not accept completely her authoritarian ways. She would try to break them, psychologically, and if this failed she would create a huge scene and expel the miscreants, though she usually readmitted them. These scenes did not occur as often as in the rumors about the Handy Colony. Lowney was usually calm and supportive, talking knowingly about the work of her students. She made them believe they were going to succeed.

Over the years, she had developed into a skilled editor. Although her methods of teaching writing were unorthodox, her editorial advice was traditional. She read through manuscripts carefully and made notes in her typical scrawl. She admired Thomas Uzzell's excellent text, *The Technique of the Novel*, and incorporated his ideas into her editorial work. As she read student fiction, she was interested in plot, dialogue, conflict, character development, point of view, mood, style. She was concerned about the necessity to "write truth — don't falsify facts" ("Colony Writing Manual" 12, UIS). She recommended Uzzell's book to Jones and other students, and she compiled a fifty-four-page "Colony Writing Manual," which owes a large debt to Uzzell's work. Our examination of colonists' manuscripts marked up by Lowney indicates that she generally gave good advice about problems in the work and suggested ways to strengthen it. Hidden beneath her eccentric ways were her qualities as a shrewd editor. She did make mistakes, but when her editorial work is considered in its entirety, it was largely successful.

The contractor who built Jim's house turned him on to motorcycle riding, which helped him get away from distractions. There was even horseplay with the motorcycles. Once Jim and Lowney's brother Andy rode their machines into Andy's mother's parlor. The two young men thought it a great joke. She did not.

From 1950 to 1957 the pattern was set: Lowney managed the colony during the warm months, took a few of the colonists with her and Jim to Florida or Arizona during the cold months, often leaving two students or so in Marshall to live with Harry's mother during the winter months. Stories both favorable and unfavorable appeared about the colony. Jim struggled with *Some Came Running*, faced as he was with the burden of writing a second book after the huge success of his first.

One shattering event for Jim took place in June 1952. His sister, Mary Ann, then only twenty-seven years old, was living at the colony and working on *The Third Time You Killed Me*. Lowney, busy with the colony, and Jim, working on another novel, were not fully aware of Mary Ann's health problems and she died of a seizure one night. Her unfinished novel is in the Handy Collection at the University of Illinois at Springfield and shows that she had definite literary promise. Their uncle Charlie Jones, who hated Lowney and disliked the colony and his nephew's involvement with it, tried to cause trouble. He requested that the nearest U.S. marshall investigate the circumstances of his niece's death and asked for an inquest. There was a trial, and the jury decided Mary Ann died of natural causes. Jim finally broke all ties with his uncle (MacShane 127–28).

6
Real Life and Fiction at the Colony

In 1952 and 1953 the colony was well established: buildings were in place, sidewalks were in, and the swimming pool was finished. About twenty colonists were in attendance in 1952 and about fifteen in 1953. Some returned every year, others did not last a season. We have selected three case studies to illustrate the comings and goings of colonists.

John Bowers

John Bowers learned about Lowney from Whipple's *Life* article, and he came to the colony in the summer of 1952. He had read *From Here to Eternity* the year before, when he was a senior at the University of Tennessee. That novel, he recalled in *The Colony*, "had made me feel like a man, and in a way had made me thereafter see everything in a slightly different light" (6). Lowney made him feel wanted, encouraged him, praised him to other colonists, but Bowers was never quite a true believer. Jokingly, she referred to him as kinfolk, and he, proud of his education and his bookish family, did not want to be known as a hillbilly (Sackrider narrative). Still, he stayed on, and for a long time he clung to the hope that the novel he wrote in his two sessions at the colony (1952 and 1953) would be a success. This belief persisted long after he left the Marshall grounds, but he quickly recognized how quixotic Lowney's actions were. He eventually came to doubt her easy optimism, her belief that she could teach anyone to write. In his fictionalized book about her and the Handy Colony, she appears faintly ridiculous with her occult beliefs, her dietary restrictions, her insistence on the efficacy of enemas. Lowney's best qualities are largely missing in Bowers's account.

In *The Colony*, he shows Lowney, Jim, and Harry in action as well as the interrelationships of the diverse colonists themselves, many of whom were misfits who wanted to be writers, who believed that Lowney would show them the way to success, just as she had led and badgered Jim to fame and fortune. Bowers was a dissident, in 1952–1953 at least, a sharp observer of the slightly comic events around them but still a believer in his own talent and his novel. And he remained partially under her spell. What she said in praise of the Democratic party, on the perfidy of women, about Hemingway, "found a fertile virgin field in my unused Tennessee mind," he wrote. Still, he did not disagree when another dissident cried out, "Fuck the Masters of the Far East. Bunch of loony shit if I ever heard it." Another screamed, "And to hell with enemas. My asshole can't take it no more!" (*Colony* 214). Still, Bowers stayed on.

By the end of the second year, his novel was almost finished, but he delayed writing the last scenes. He envisioned having to compose the necessary tribute to Lowney, a set piece expected of all colonists. He feared that his novel might make money, and Lowney would possess him physically and financially as she did Jim, who had built his house just on the edge of the colony grounds. Lowney wanted Bowers to buy land nearby and build his house there. She would go on controlling his life. With Lowney's prodding, Bowers did contrive an ending to his novel. His hero dropped out of college, abandoned his home and the ideas passed on to him, and played his guitar "for peanuts in a beer joint." Bowers then had "him discovered (à la Hollywood) by a shrewd agent who gleaned his potential. Not so hard. A few crisp scenes, leaving much blessedly to suggestion, should do it" (*Colony* 219). The novel was completed and handed to Lowney.

Bowers wrote:

> I sat on the edge of my bunk, feeling nothing, staring at the floor, waiting for the first surge of happiness to hit me at the thought of the task all finished, the privations and agonies ended. Only to hear Lowney's scream in the night. "Johnny, come here. Come here this second." She half-threw, half-handed me the pile of manuscript. "This won't do. You've wrapped everything up too arbitrarily, too slickly. It happens in life that way, but it can't in fiction. You must leave the impression in fiction that everything happens by a Grand Design, that nothing happens by chance or due to fickleness. Go do this ending again." (225)

He did it in a week and a half.

Lowney read the manuscript again, and although she thought the conclusion "could be better," she was ready to allow *The Thirst of Youth* to be mailed to a New York agent. "Well," that enormous white smile breaking, "congratulations. I knew you could do it," she told him.

Bowers quickly said his good-byes.

"Take care of yourself and don't hitch up with an idiot woman," Lowney told him. "We'll see you soon. Anytime. You can always come back."

"Be seeing you, buddy," Jim said. "Keep your pecker in your pants!" (225–26)

Lowney remained optimistic, but the agent could not sell the novel. Bowers's second novel, written away from the Handy Colony, did not sell either. After pumping gas, driving a cab, working as a shill in a casino, and holding several other jobs, he became an editor and a professional writer, author of *The Colony, Stonewall Jackson: Portrait of a Soldier*, and many other works. He did not publish *The Colony* until 1971, well after Lowney's death in 1964. It was easier for him to publish explicit sexual scenes than it had been for Jones, and the novel also describes his having sex with a girlfriend in Tennessee and with whores in Terre Haute while he was at the colony.

Don Sackrider believes that John Bowers caught the situation comedy aspects of the colony, but he did not know Jim, Lowney, and Harry well enough to present them as people. His mocking tone was an effective literary device but distorts the truth of these three people and the institution they brought into being.

Almost twenty years after Bowers published *The Colony*, he wrote the preface to *James Jones in Illinois: A Guide to the Handy Writers' Colony Collection* (1989) and remembered Lowney's overpowering personality and her quirkiness with affection. He believed that his "experience at the colony has proven pivotal in my life—although I did not realize it at the time." Lowney and Jim ("a bona fide, 100% writer") and Bowers's two years at the colony saved him from the conventional middle-class life that had been laid out for him. The comedy of *The Colony* is put aside in this preface, and Bowers concludes: "I'll never know the person I might have become if not for Lowney Handy. Stilled forever now are the possibilities I left behind. I would still have been a writer—I'm certain—but not, for good or bad, the one I am" (xi).

Don Sackrider

Don was the first student Lowney brought into her orbit after working several years with Jim. He came to her after finishing high school and at a time before the Handy Colony was formally organized. He was a colonist, served briefly in the army, and then returned to the colony. At first he had too little experience and was too close to the events to deal with the subject of his fiction—his break with Nita. Later, he wrote what he considered a good story, "To Spite Your Own Face," based roughly on observations when he was in the army, a story vetted by both Lowney and Jim, but which did not sell. When he returned to the colony he was a general factotum, a favorite of Lowney's, intrigued by her eclectic philosophies, truly a dedicated follower. He had a major problem. He had writer's block "just because we were there," Don now thinks. He believes he was too caught up in building a colony and what was going on in the world of Jim and Lowney. He was afraid to cut his losses, let go, turn to other things. Jim had decided that Don was not going to become a writer, and Lowney had come to that conclusion also. She kept offering Don ways out of the colony trap he was in, and he kept refusing to escape (Sackrider narrative).

In the summer of 1953, however, there was a confrontation over food he picked up for Lowney and Jim at Tom's Restaurant in Marshall. Lowney had told Don to ask for turkey and dressing with gravy and no side dishes. The waitress at Tom's was unable to visualize why anyone would not take the works when it cost the same anyway, and after five minutes of trying to explain Lowney's explicit order, Don took pity on the waitress and told her to do it her way. Lowney was furious when Don arrived with the extra food. As he tried to explain, Jim began to berate him. Finally Don said to them, "If you don't like it, go get your own food." Lowney and Jim continued to protest, and Don finally said "fuck you" and walked out.

Lowney came to his cabin and said if he did not admit he was wrong and apologize he had to leave the colony. He refused. He now thinks that all three of them knew that, after six years with them and no book in sight, it was time for him to be on his own, away from them.

Harry arrived and tried to get Don to square things with Lowney. Don did not. Once Harry left Don's barracks room, Don fought back his tears, packed his few belongings, and with no money walked through Mrs. Handy's yard to Route 40 and put up his thumb. It was almost sundown by the time he reached the highway. The big maples and elms on the Handy Colony grounds emphasized the security he was leaving behind. He could not go to Robinson, for too much would need explaining. He made his way to Fort Riley, Kansas, where his brother Arden was stationed. Arden and his wife, Maggie (who had grown up across the street from Lowney), took him in and nurtured him. For two months he tried to go on writing, then he gave it up and decided to get a job. When he had been hitchhiking through Kansas City, he had thought, "I would sure hate to be stuck in this place." But there he was in Kansas, just as Dorothy in *The Wizard of Oz* had been. He applied for a job at TWA and gave Harry Handy as a reference, saying he had worked for Harry as his private secretary at the oil refinery. Harry backed up Don's story, and eight weeks after leaving the Handy Colony, Don had the airline job in the TWA home office in Kansas City.

Because Lowney quickly forgot her anger and her rash actions of "running-off" colonists, Don thinks he could have gone back to the colony after his absence of two months and would have been welcomed once again into the fold. He now says, "I was as low as I had ever been in my life, but I knew that if I went back I would be even lower."

Don worked in the TWA headquarters at the airport in Kansas City. He was paid $250 a month, enough for him to start flying lessons, supplemented by some small support from the GI Bill. True to her philosophy of tearing prospective writers down in order to rebuild them, Lowney consistently tried to destroy the ego of her students, and she had managed to destroy Don's self-confidence. Only when he did well in flight training and then made his first solo flight did he begin to believe in himself again. He had no contact with Lowney for several years, but eventually the breach in their relationship was healed. Don had a long and well-paid career as a commercial pilot and is now retired, living in Florida, Washington, and Europe.

Looking back at the good times and bad times with Lowney, Don says: "I have no regrets in leaving the Colony. It had to be done. I had become increasingly inhibited by the specter of Lowney always there no matter where she was. Maybe I would not have the good life I now live if I had never met her. . . . I'm not sorry I did not become an actor, for the uncertainties of that profession are enormous. And I would not like having to live an old age without money." Lowney often said she had to cause pain for the good of her students.

Don also reestablished friendly relations with Jim, who would ask Don, "Are you still writing?" Don would always reply, "No, but I'm having fun."

David Ray

In 1952–1953, Don regarded John Bowers as a Tennessee Rebel. At first, Don remembers, he resented the insurrectionists' disloyalty to Lowney. Ultimately, he just listened and let them blow off steam. David Ray not only blew off steam during the month he was at the Handy Colony—he also wrote damning articles about the colony, taking direct aim at Lowney's most vulnerable spots.

Ray's longest account of his experiences with Lowney and Jim was "Mrs. Handy's Curious Colony," published in the *Chicago Magazine* in September 1956. Ray had done his undergraduate work at the University of Chicago and graduated in 1952. He applied for a scholarship to pursue graduate work there but was turned down because of poor grades caused by his concentrating on his own writing and his incessant participation in intellectual discussions with his fellow students. He became an intellectual-in-exile at the University of Arizona, "where there were enough good courses in English to occupy one semester's work." Just as he was running out of courses to take, he read that James Jones was in Tucson, staying at a trailer park. Ray and two fellow writers called on Jim, whom he described as "a barrel-chested fellow dressed in levis and a stack of turquoise bracelets." Jim immediately drew the three into a discussion of Thomas Wolfe, Theodore Dreiser, and James Jones. Ray had read some Wolfe but was far from being an admirer. In his article, he wrote that he "discoursed wildly, challenged by Jones' status into a duel-to-the-death battle of wits, predestined to defeat by the fact of his fame" (23).

In defeat, Ray produced one of his manuscripts and asked Jones to look it over. Jim promised to read it and "to show it to Lowney," explaining that Lowney was "a woman of depth and integrity" and that "she taught me everything I know about writing" (23). He urged Ray to write Lowney in Robinson. The response came from Tucson, for she had brought three colonists to warmer climes for the winter and had moved into a house there. She told Ray that his two friends would not receive her help because they had not written her nor had they brought manuscripts for Jim to read. Ray found that his defense of his friends was brushed aside. Still, Lowney liked his story and requested him to visit her.

Lowney asked several questions at the beginning of their session: Did he want to become a great writer? Was he willing to work? Naturally his response was yes. She then assured him that he "was a natural" (his later career shows how right she was) and that she could turn him into a great writer just as she had done Jim. She next asked him to make three wishes, "which she would grant with her mental magic wand." Ray's account appears to exaggerate the truth: "The only price I had to pay for the fulfillment of the wishes (only one of which had to be the great writer idea; the other two could be anything in the world) was complete devotion to her orders (she called them 'commandments'); sacrifice of all personal possessions, including human relationships; the endurance of a copy program (copying verbatim 'works of the masters' which she assigned), and a large percentage of all eventual royalties" (24).

While this summary has many elements of truth, she did not demand a large part of the royalties of colonists who published. Instead, she asked 10 percent, a reasonable percentage considering students paid no fees at the colony and Lowney acted as an unofficial agent in the attempt to find a publisher.

Lowney could cast an initial spell on even a University of Chicago intellectual. Ray, though, began to have doubts as he met with Lowney and the three colonists she had with her. He thought her pronouncements innocuous and anti-intellectual (she railed against T. S. Eliot). At her house, Ray told Lowney he had decided he did not want to go to the colony, and the two had a "violent argument" (24). In his article, Ray comes across as being as argumentative as Lowney, and Lowney took the challenge. Ray left Lowney's rented house and returned to his rooming house. Three hours later Jim and Lowney appeared. Lowney apologized, told him he was ready for the colony, that he needed her and her system. She gave him a hard luck story about all the money she was spending on the colony and assured him she could get him an advance from a publisher within twelve months. Lowney managed to recast her spell, but it soon faded because of her authoritarian ways.

When it was time at the end of the winter season in Arizona to return to Marshall and the opening of the Handy Colony, Lowney decreed that Ray and another "apprentice" writer should ride in the back seat. He was learning that Lowney believed in the caste system; apprentices did not belong in the front seat of famous writer Jones's Chrysler.

At the colony, Ray was immediately unhappy. He did not fit in with many colonists, who decided he was a snob. He mocked the food and was incensed by Lowney's anti-intellectualism. In his report, her contraband writers included "Proust (pronounced 'Prowst'), Wallace Stevens (pronounced Walter Stevens), Kafka (pronounced 'Kafkia'), Dylan Thomas (pronounced 'Die-lane Thompson')." Lowney was indeed self-taught and given in some instances to misinterpretation of literary works and mispronunciation of the names of literary legends. She was sometimes homophobic. She snatched one of Proust's novels from Ray and threw it away with these words, "That's one queer we don't need around here" ("Mrs. Handy's Curious Colony" 26).

Ray is correct in pointing out that many of Lowney's opinions—actually pronouncements—came from Madame Blavatsky, Annie Besant, Paul Brunton, Somerset Maugham's *The Razor's Edge*, and Emerson, but in his mocking of Lowney's New Age beliefs he could not see how occult and Eastern philosophical ideas had played an important part in nineteenth- and twentieth-century American literature. Ray did not see that Lowney had studied these texts carefully and was a true believer. Ray reported that he tried to adjust to the Spartan living arrangements, to Jim's egotistical ways, to sexual deprivations (though there were rumors of a trip to the whorehouse in Terre Haute to relieve tensions), to Lowney's platitudes and quirky literary judgments, to her many mispronunciations, but the atmosphere in Marshall was even more crackpot than it had been in Tucson. He came to believe that he and the other colonists were living in "physical and emotional poverty" (26) at a time when Jim and Lowney were ostentatiously enjoying the fruits of the wealth from sales of *From Here to Eternity*.

The defining moment came when three of his friends from the University of Chicago arrived for a visit. At first the encounter between the Chicago intellectuals and the Handy Colony was comic. The friends knew Ray was at the colony but did not know where it was. They had read Whipple's article and made their way to the Handy house in Robinson. Harry told them he could not even tell them where the colony was without Lowney's permission and called Lowney, who agreed they could visit the next morning.

Ray was then subjected to one of Lowney's harangues. She insisted he had broken the rules and invited his friends for a visit. Ray made the mistake of defending himself, of pointing out that the three had gone to Robinson instead of Marshall, but this undoubtedly just angered Lowney more. She then called out a long list of his transgressions: making contact with the outside world by writing letters, reading Proust, asking too many questions, not typing enough.

Jim participated in the farcical scenes. The next morning at six o'clock, when Ray was having his instant coffee in the ramada, Jim arrived to take him to Lowney's house, where she told him to observe his friends closely for they would be "good material" for his later fiction. Indeed, they were good material—but for the articles he wrote about the Handy Colony, not for his fiction. He waited for his friends to arrive on the steps of Lowney's house, located just inside the gate. When they came walking up the lane, he knew the coming scenes were going to be dangerous, for together they encapsulated several of Lowney's oft-stated hatreds:

> Eyeglasses. She had thrown Ray's away the first day he spent
>   at the colony, giving him a copy of Aldous Huxley's *Sight*
>   *Without Glasses.*
> A beret. Clearly the sign of an intellectual.
> A beard. The colonists wore their hair neatly trimmed and facial
>   hair was forbidden.

Ray envisioned Lowney's swift attack, breaking of glasses, destruction of beret, sudden scissoring of the beard, but instead she invited Ray and his visitors into her living room. At first she was charming. Then her mood suddenly changed, and she demanded they confess that they had really made the trip to meet Jones. They had to agree it was true.

Lowney then did what Ray had feared she would do: she turned to the hated glasses, beret, and beard. She recognized the bearded one as the ringleader and demanded of him:

"Do you know why people wear glasses?"

The three replied in unison, "No."

Lowney then looked for an occult book to provide the answer.

What happened next was high comedy: "In doing so . . . she reached for her own glasses. Such a stock vaudeville improbability elicited an involuntary chuckle" from one of his friends. The laughter angered Lowney, but she quickly resumed her more charming personality. She then asked who they considered were great writers. One ventured D. H. Lawrence.

Ray knew what was going to happen, for Lowney had a theory known to the colonists that homosexuals were obsessed with sex and their "dissipations" led to bad health and tuberculosis. She presented the theory to the incredulous visitors: "D. H. Lawrence was a queer, and that's why he died from T.B.— I know why people get T.B."

One of the three rashly told her she was wrong. Lowney was enraged. She shouted at them: "You get out of here. You can't come in here with your goddamned intellectual claptrap and take up my time."

She rushed them toward the door of her house and ordered Ray to pack and leave the colony. Lowney being Lowney, she abruptly changed course and called Jim to show the beard, the beret, and the four eyes around the grounds.

The three engaged one of the colonists on a subject Jim obviously would not object to: "What do you do for sex around here?"

A nameless colonist responded, "Well, about once a month me and some of the boys take a trip over to Terre Haute. They have a good deal over there for ten dollars a piece."

"That's a little impersonal, isn't it?" the beard or the beret or the four eyes responded.

The answer was one Lowney approved. "That's the way I like it. No personal *involvements* that way. No emotions."

While this conversation was taking place, Ray reappeared with his packed bag.

"Where are you going?" Lowney demanded.

"You told me to leave."

Lowney told him that she had changed her mind and he should unpack. He wanted to leave with his friends, but she shouted: "You can't leave."

She then shouted to his friends, "What do you [expletives deleted by Ray to protect the gentle readers of *Chicago*] mean taking up Jones' time? He's a busy man. His time means money."

Lowney often bragged of running off erring colonists, and this time she literately threw the three out. She began throwing bricks at them. One was slower than the others, and a brick hit him in the back.

"Lady," he called to her, "I've got a sore foot, I can't run."

She threw another brick. He ran.

Jim stood and watched, laughing.

As hot blooded as her Kentucky ancestors, Lowney was not content. She rushed to her car and drove off after the three running down the lane. By now Jim was trying to get her to stop. Accelerating quickly, she almost ran the visitors down. She stopped and ordered them into the car, announcing in her sweetest voice that she was just testing them. That mood changed quickly, for she escorted them several miles out of town and put them out, saying they could walk back to Marshall. They began the trek.

Lowney returned, loaded them in the car again, and took them into town, where she located the police chief, who just happened to be her father.

"Take these [expletive deleted by Ray] and throw them in jail till the bus to Chicago leaves, Dad."

"Sure," was his response, and Ray rightly concluded that Lowney was proving her frequent boast: "I run this town."

One of the three told Lowney that his father was a prominent attorney, and she once again changed course.

"All right then," she told her father, "take them to the bus station and guard them and put them on that bus."

The three telephoned Ray from the bus station, offering to buy him a ticket to Chicago. "No dice," she told Ray. Jim told Ray not to be upset, but to get back to work "because if he could (being a great man) I certainly could" ("Mrs. Handy's Curious Colony" 25–27).

For two weeks, Lowney refused to allow Ray to leave. Finally, on the day Montgomery Clift—who played Prewitt in the film version of *From Here to Eternity*—was to arrive, Ray approached Lowney again, this time somewhat menacingly, for he carried a hammer he had been using to clean mortar off some used bricks. Some visitors had come to the colony, hoping to see and meet Clift, and Lowney did not want to make a public scene, so she agreed for Ray to depart. Lowney was all sweetness at his leaving, but Jim "shook hands with a reprimanding look of disappointment" (27). No "Keep your pecker in your pants" for intellectual troublemaker Ray.

Ray wrote in his journal during his stay at the colony: "It's impossible to leave here openly, because once you tell her you want to leave she starts a tirade and in two minutes proves to you with sheer violence that one can't possibly become a writer any place in the world but here." Ray concluded that "Lowney's forte is this ability to control people, and all of her devotees share a belief that she has the power of God" ("Mrs. Handy's Curious Colony" 27).

Don believes that Ray was exaggerating Lowney's control over his leaving. He thinks Lowney had admitted Ray to see if she could change him and control him, and she was being her usual authoritarian self. However, Lowney was not always around, and Don never saw her restrain anyone from leaving. All Ray had to do was walk across the bridge to Mrs. Handy's property fronting the Cumberland Road, put out his thumb, and get a ride out of Marshall, as Don himself did.

Lowney was concerned about the lives and creative work of the colonists. At times she was also mistaken and misguided. She should have found a better way to send Don away from the colony, to encourage him to get on with his life and to find a career outside of writing. She had helped him at crucial times during his late adolescence, but she always had more control over him than was good for his development. Bowers, the Tennessee Rebel, fared better than Don or David Ray, for he did write his novel, though it appears that Lowney gave him bad advice about the revision of the ending. Lowney, Jim, and the summer campers in Marshall furnished Bowers with superb material for his evocative fictionalized work, *The Colony*.

At first, Lowney gave David Ray the same high praise she sometimes gave to Don and John Bowers, but Ray was more overt in his rebellion than Bowers was. Lowney often struck the pose of an anti-intellectual in both actions and words. In many ways, though, she was an intellectual. She was interested in many ideas, she was a constant reader, but she was self-taught and her reading was limited in range. Most important, she was an authoritarian who held tenaciously to some outrageous beliefs. If Ray's friends had told Lowney that their favorite American authors were ones she admired, Lowney would have engaged them in a long conversation and would have concluded that the University of Chicago was doing right by its students.

Certainly, the comic scene in which she threw bricks at the friends of Ray is a disturbing one, one that easily could have happened on the frontier and then been written about by Longstreet or other frontier humorists. The cruelty in this farce should not be lost on anyone studying the remarkable careers of Lowney and Jim. Jim to outsiders presented a macho, sometime anti-intellectual picture of himself, but this was mostly facade. He had wide intellectual and artistic interests. He was at his worst when he laughed at Lowney's attacks on the beard, the beret, and the glasses (his own pair having been much missed when he was wounded on Guadalcanal) and when he went along with the caste system Lowney imposed at the colony, while escaping most of the rules himself.

David Ray managed to anger Jim. Ray pointed out in the *Chicago Magazine* article that Jones in *Eternity* drew heavily on episodes in Wolfe's *Of Time and the River,* John Dos Passos's *U.S.A.,* Norman Mailer's *The Naked and the Dead,* Hemingway's *For Whom the Bell Tolls,* F. Scott Fitzgerald's *The Great Gatsby,* and James Joyce's *Ulysses.* He asserts: "It is true that certain passages in Jones' book appear almost identical not only in style but in content to parts of novels which he 'copied' on his typewriter for more than seven years" (27). Jim did far less copying of prescribed works than later colonists did, though Ray reports he saw Jim's personal copy of *For Whom the Bell Tolls* with the note in chapter 37 "Copy for Warden-Karen love scenes." Ray is certainly right in the larger sense: the novels he mentioned—and others such as *The Grapes of Wrath*—did influence Jim, and he does adapt stylistic and plot materials from them. Lowney's copying method certainly had its dangers.

Jim was angered by Ray's assertions about the Handy Colony and by his charges against him. He wrote Kenneth Hawkins, his attorney in Chicago, to see if anything could be done about Ray's article (Garrett 113). No action was taken.

Many of the stories about Lowney emphasize how determined and autocratic she was. They stress her failures and not her successes, her eccentricities and foibles, not her strengths. There are other stories about Lowney at her best: her encouragement of her students, her quiet times with the colonists as she spun out humorous stories, her generosity, her demanding work as an editor. These aspects of Lowney are elusive but important in reaching a balanced understanding of her.

The summer of 1953, when Don left the colony, there was a brewing rebellion against the discipline imposed by Lowney. Don believes Bowers and Ray were the leaders of the dissidents, and he was appalled at the irreverence toward the warden of the colony. The rebellious believed that Lowney could make them into famous writers as she had Jones, but they were resentful of not being Jones and of being treated like privates.

Jim Jones's *Some Came Running*

Meanwhile, Jim was making slow progress on his next novel, *Some Came Running*. The winter of 1952–1953, when Lowney and Jim were in Tucson (the winter David Ray was recruited), Harry was back in Illinois overseeing the planning and building of Jim's bachelor house just outside the colony gate.

Even though Jim was far away in Arizona, he still found the construction process troublesome. There were also constant emotional problems with Lowney, and at times he became entangled in the lives of the colonists. There was an even greater problem as he wrote Burroughs Mitchell, his editor at Scribner's, on July 31, 1953: "I fear I've lost my drive *to* write because of being successful. I fear I've lost my ability to really like people. Oh, shit I could go on by the hour. And then, on the other hand, I'm afraid that in my desire to *be* able to like people, I'm inclined not only to wind up making everything untrue to people, but also sentimental" (*To Reach Eternity* 195). Jim moved around his trailer, drinking hobo coffee, pondering his next novel, sitting at the typewriter to get some words down, making a second martini after lunch.

Jim was struggling with many problems in what he originally called his "Russ" (Meskimen) novel. He was intrigued by Russ and Arkie, one a writer manqué, the other a professional gambler. In the novel Jim stayed close to the essential outlines of each of their lives, picturing them as renegades, as inhabiting the lower depths of midwestern American life.

Jim had written about Russ and Arkie in "None Sing So Wildly," but he had grown disenchanted with this early presentation of two of the central characters in his new novel. He had originally believed they were capable of integrity, but now he doubted it. Jim wrote Mitchell that if he had written Prewitt and Warden in *From Here to Eternity* just as they were he "wouldnt have had any story." In actuality, "When Prew went to the Stockades, he just came out and went right back to the life he'd been living. . . . Somehow in his mind, he excused himself out of something, so that his integrity was never really put to the supreme test, as it was in the book" (*To Reach Eternity* 194).

In his first story about Russ and Arkie, he had romanticized them. He had come to the conclusion, though, that "actually they were just a couple of bums." He had to find a new way to deal with these renegades on the out-skirts of small-town life, he told Mitchell: "Because to write them as they really are would be so depressing, not only to me, but to readers, that I wouldnt have any book—or any plot either" (*To Reach Eternity* 194). He had not solved his artistic problems in 1953 and was "scared as hell" (195).

Real Life and Fiction at the Colony

The easy part was creating the characters from real counterparts. He wrote these notes about Russ Meskimen (Dave Hirsh of the novel) and his girlfriend, Katie (the name is spelled both "Katie" and "Katy" in various letters written by Lowney and Jim; she is Ginnie in the novel):

> Lowney said to Russ in car, coming home from Lake Lawrence, "If you'll do what I tell you I'll make a whale of a team out of the both of you. But neither one of you is ready to get married yet because neither one of you has learned your lesson yet. Society would hook both of you, the way you both think now, and when society hooks a writer there aint no writer any more."
>
> Russ, who had spent six or eight years in Hollywood (living with his sister and where, he says, he wrote dialogue for movies) where he was strongly influenced by a writer named John Fante, has been living here for three yrs, since he was flown home from Europe and discharged. Mainly because he was disillusioned by Hollywood and the "artistic" life, and by Fante's selling out for money as a screen writer. [Russ returned to Robinson and for] three years [there had] been a continuous round of drunks and sex bouts with Katie, "professionally" gambling at the Moose (in which the first year was a big financial success, and the last two complete flops, so that he had been living in Lincoln Hotel from hand to mouth mostly on the money Katie made as a waitress then later working in [the] new shoe factory), so Tinks Howe says. . . .
>
> Then Lowney offered him free the cabin Harry rented at Shackamack for us for a month this summer, if he would write. He could take some liquor even, and take Katie with him. Russ agreed, a little shocked that anybody would give away valuable things so off handedly. And Katie agreed. But her main point in talking to Lowney, was that Russ ought to marry her. With which Lowney disagreed because it would hamstring Russ to respectability, because obviously Katie wanted a bourgouise home and Russ to support her.
>
> But then Russ suddenly refused to take it after all, and spent a deal of time breaking down the faith in Lowney that Katie, who was very self conscious of her lack of education, had placed in her.
>
> The upshot was that Katie wrote to a one-armed vet in Ohio who had once lived with her and had been writing her to marry him and took him up. He came here, they were married, and left for Ohio.
>
> Since then Russ has been walking on the edge of a razor, about to fall off on either side. For over a week now. And we have been carrying him, talking to him, trying to get him to write which is what he says he always wanted. But now the main reason he's working on this story is because he wants to send a copy to Katie and show her how he had improved, but also show her in the story (which is about the effect upon him of her leaving) how pitiful he is without her.
>
> Hence the conversation above, when every now and then he harks back to whether Katie will ever come back or not. But he will not yet face the obvious fact that it was as much Katy's fault as his own. He is now romanticizing her into fitting the picture of the Ideal Woman he

has always carried, and which of course no woman can ever measure up to. But when Lowney or I try to kick this out from under him, he balks and will not accept the true picture. He prefers, at present, to castigate himself, to wallow in his grief and guilt. The only thing then is to have him write to show to Katie, hoping that in doing that and in getting praise he will gradually shift the motive around to writing to publish, or even writing to write.

Lowney has gone to his brother Ted [Frank Hirsh in the novel] and secured a pension for him of $60 a month, which Ted who I have never liked because of what he stood for, was more than willing to donate. Which goes to show you how often [I am wrong]. (notes to *Some Came Running*, UIS)[1]

Russ did some writing, or at least pretended to. He told his brother he was all but finished with a novel. Lowney was not working with Russ and could not confirm the story. The novel never appeared.

Katie did return, and her one-armed husband came back for her. In fact and in fiction, Katie did divorce her husband and marry Russ, but the one-armed ex-husband did not kill Russ (as he does kill Dave at the end of Jim's novel).

Robinson is a small, close-knit community, and over the years the people there talked about the Meskimen family. Some of what they said was clearly gossip. Jim turned some of these stories into his fictional presentation of Russ (Dave) and Katie (Ginnie) and other citizens, outcasts, and leading lights, in the novel.

Rumor in Robinson had it that Russ (like Dave) did leave town with some other young men when a young woman they had been sleeping with found she was pregnant. One man stayed behind and married the pregnant woman, and it turned out to be a good marriage. It was generally believed that the wrong one stayed and that Russ was the father. Tinks Howe remembers a short story Russ wrote about a character who returned home some years after a similar situation had taken place. The character would walk past the house in the evenings when the father was home from work and feel remorse to see the family life he had never had. Tinks does not know what happened to the story (it is not in the Handy collection at the University of Illinois at Springfield), and he does not remember how it ended (Howe narrative).

Gossip in Robinson also confirms Jim's account that Lowney, who believed Russ had potential as a writer, was opposed to the marriage of Russ and Katie. Katie's personal and sexual history was well known to Tinks Howe and some of his friends and was reported to Jim Jones, who used those stories in his fictional presentation of her in *Some Came Running*.

Russ Meskimen's father (according to the Robinson rumor mills) had indeed run away with a doctor's wife and had returned to town without her, just as presented in the novel. Russ's brother, owner of a furniture store (not a jewelry store as in the novel), is believed to have been presented in the novel much as he was. He was a successful businessman who—rumor had it—always had at least one girlfriend on the side, and often more. Local girls would not work for him, it was said, for their mothers would not let them. He thought he was fooling everyone in his seemingly discreet assignations but most people in Robinson knew exactly what was happening. His wife, it was said, enjoyed his money and his social position, but every now and then she would rein him in. It was also rumored that Ted employed a housekeeper who had been with the family for many years, but (unlike Old Jane in the novel) he had an ongoing affair with her, and she kept thinking he would make an honest woman of her.[2]

Ted, the prosperous Meskimen, did have a daughter, who in the novel has a first affair with Wally Dennis. Jim in the novel hardly deviated from the real Willard (Willie) Lindsay at all in this portrayal, but the affair with the Meskimen daughter was fictional. Jim shows the young, spoiled, talented Willie as he was. Willie was a favorite of Lowney's, and Jim knew him well and obviously felt that Willie would not object to his characterization in the novel. Willie was not happy, however. Lowney later remarked to Don: "How would you feel if someone killed you off in their book?" (Sackrider narrative).

The second major male character in *Some Came Running* was Bama Dillert, based on Grover Douglas Ashby, called "Arkie" by all his friends. Arkie came to Robinson in 1934 with his mother, brother, and sisters. His father did not come up from Arkansas until later. In the depth of the depression, the mother supported the family by taking in laundry, raising chickens, gardening, and doing housework for more affluent families. She was a self-sufficient, religious woman who sent her children to church every Sunday. Arkie was self-sufficient in his own way too; he put his nickel in his pocket and not in the offering. He married a farm girl who lived not far from Robinson, and she remained on the farm while he was away in the army. When he returned from military service, he never held a job (slight correction: he was said to have worked one morning at the refinery). He left his wife and children at the farm and spent his days and nights gambling. He played cards, pool, horses, and any game found in the numerous taverns. He was a champion shuffleboard player. He could and did bet on anything. Even when drunk he was a better cardplayer and pool player than most. Tinks Howe played in many poker games with Arkie and felt that, except for himself, Arkie was the best cardplayer he knew. There were always marked decks around the clubs, and Arkie never drank so much that he could not read the backs of the cards.

He was well liked by women but was discreet in his many affairs. He was a soft touch for some of the women at the clubs who would lose money in the slot machines and then worry about what their husbands would say when they went home. He frequently would give them money, and they would pay him back with money or with sex.

Arkie called Tinks one Sunday and asked to borrow two hundred dollars. He wanted to bail out a woman he knew who had been picked up for being drunk. Tinks said, "I didn't know you were interested in Betty."

"I'm not," Arkie replied, "but no one should spend the night in jail and a woman sure shouldn't." Tinks gave him the money, and it was repaid the next week (Howe narrative).

Jim picked up the many stories in Robinson about Arkie and his hat. When his nephew was a young boy staying at his grandmother Ashby's house, Arkie would come in late, get up late, and go to the bathroom wearing his Stetson hat, his boxer shorts, and his shoes. When he fell over unconscious at the American Legion in Robinson, he awoke as the ambulance crew was taking him out, asked for his hat, and went out with it on his chest. Bama and his hat are presented comically in the novel.

Arkie was an alcoholic (like Bama). When a doctor in the veterans' hospital asked him if he drank too much, he responded, "Well, not too much; perhaps a fifth a day or so."

Helen Howe says that when Arkie was sick and drunk in his shabby hotel room in Robinson, she would prepare food for him and try to get him to eat and sober up and get control of his body again. He would get himself into terrible shape. Even Tinks would have to intervene on occasion. Arkie was a diabetic (like Bama) and his liver was almost finished. Helen says that Arkie always cleaned up his act and his mouth when he was around women, and he was careful about the way he talked when the Howe children were around (Howe narrative).

About a year before his death in 1970, Arkie was in a fight at the American Legion. He was drunk and was accused of cheating (ironically, he was not cheating that time), was beaten up and suffered a broken ankle. This was in February, it was cold, and he needed a toe cover for his cast. Helen bought wool yarn and made him three, one navy, one black, and one brown. Arkie, a gambler with social graces, greatly appreciated Helen's gifts. Helen comments:

> Arkie was personable and friendly to others and was liked by most. However, he didn't like many people very well and trusted even fewer. The young men in the community thought he was "cool" and liked to hang around with him. He would show them pool shots and [teach them] how to be a star. He also loaned them money, took their part when it was necessary, and tried to keep them on the right path. He was a gambler; he was known to always have an edge; he was a heavy drinker; but he was much more than this. He was a loyal and loved friend who would go to any lengths to help if you needed him. He never pretended to be anything he wasn't. Arkie's daughter said, "Daddy left me three things when he died: a deck of marked cards, a pair of loaded dice, and his Good Conduct Medal." This was Arkie! (Howe narrative)

Jim knew Arkie, but not as intimately as Helen and Tinks did; Tinks furnished Jim story material about Arkie and his ways for inclusion in the novel. In Helen's opinion, Jim also wrote some of himself and Tinks into the character of Arkie. Helen can identify the large number of Robinsonians who appear in *Some Came Running* in sometimes barely disguised form. She also can list the bars, service clubs, factories, and nearby towns described in the novel. The influence of Thomas Wolfe in drawing characters from real life — although adding features and events that made them composite creations — is as prevalent in *Some Came Running* as in *From Here to Eternity*. It is remarkable that Jones did not face lawsuits from several Robinsonians. Certainly several were angry about the way they were presented, just as many in Asheville, North Carolina, had been incensed about their appearance in Wolfe's *Look Homeward, Angel*.

Two major characters remain to be identified here: Gwen French, creative writing teacher at the local college, and her father, Bob French. Gwen is based largely on Lowney, though it is a Lowney without dramatic mood changes and without her "copying" theories of teaching. Instead of Lowney's frigidity, her lack of interest in passionate sexual relations, Jones presents Gwen as a virgin posing as a woman of many affairs. Comically, Jones declared that Emily Dickinson inspired his characterization of Gwen.

Bob French was, according to Jones in one of his fanciful moods, influenced by the character of John Crowe Ransom. There were also some character traits drawn from Mr. English, who taught literature at Robinson High School. Mostly, though, Bob French is a portrait of Harry Handy. Lowney's beliefs in the philosophies of Madame Blavatsky and assorted Oriental beliefs have been transferred to Bob French.

Some Came Running is a long and ambitious novel. Savaged by criticism after it first appeared, the book has in recent years been reevaluated. James Giles described the novel as an honorable failure (69–90). The late Willie Morris spoke of it as "the most neglected . . . great novel of twentieth-century American literature" (*James Jones* 76–77). Steven Carter argues forcefully that the novel contains a thorough explanation of Jones's ideas on karmic relationships (132–61).

Lowney liked to intermingle quotes from the King James version of the Bible among her theosophical and Oriental and occult religious sayings, and the title of the novel comes from the Gospel of Mark, chapter 10:

> 17. And when he was gone forth into the way, there came one running, and kneeled to him, and asked him, Good Master, what shall I do that I may inherit eternal life?
> 18. And Jesus said unto him, Why callest thou me good: *there is* none good but one, *that is*, God.
> 19. Thou knowest the commandments, Do not commit adultery, Do

not kill, Do not steal, Do not bear false witness, Defraud not, Honour thy father and mother.

20. And he answered and said unto him, Master, all these have I observed from my youth.

21. Then Jesus beholding him loved him and said unto him, One thing thou lackest: go thy way, sell whatsoever thou hast, and give to the poor, and thou shalt have treasure in heaven: and come, take up the cross, and follow me.

22. And he was sad at that saying, and went away grieved: for he had great possessions.

This biblical text is the same one Lowney quoted to Don when he gave up the security afforded by his relationship with Nita to follow Lowney.

With this rubric, Jones declared that he would protest the materialism of post–World War II America. He was, then, specifically drawing upon this much ignored Christian parable. Jones was also an admirer of the works of Emerson and Thoreau with their strong anti-materialism biases. Many of the theosophical and Hindu works Lowney recommended to him were as specifically antimaterialistic as the parable of Jesus. When the novel *Some Came Running* appeared in 1957, Americans were prosperous and contented, and Jones's analysis of people adrift, self-deluded, and lost was not welcomed.

Well over half the novel is concerned with blue-collar Americans and those one notch below—the renegades, castaways, layabouts, gamblers, ne'er-do-wells. Jones also devotes significant sections to the poet-intellectual Bob French and his college teacher-critic daughter, Gwen; a local judge; and middle-class businessman Frank Hirsh with his wife and daughter. The novel is told mostly in dialogue, and Jones, in both the narrative and the dialogue, was working with what he called "colloquial forms." Garrett has written about this controversial experiment: "he means not merely the free and easy use of the living, *spoken* American idiom in dialogue or in first-person narration, but the attempt to carry it into the narrative itself, into third person narrative. . . . [it is] as if the author-narrator were speaking almost in a composite language of the characters, within the context of the characters' own verbal capacities and limitations" (116).

Some Came Running was savagely attacked by critics in 1957. Jones's experimentation with colloquial forms was misunderstood. He was accused of using bad grammar and being illiterate. In the *New Leader*, Granville Hicks wrote: "This is not just inept or careless writing, it is an assault upon the language" ("James Jones's" 22). Several of the reviewers complained that Jones did not understand the use of apostrophes and consistently used *dont*, not knowing better.

Part of the blame, it would now appear forty years later, was that Scribner's did not arrange prepublication interviews, in which Jones would talk about his experimental methods and his vision of prosperous America in the 1950s.

Instead, much of the emphasis in the prepublication stories was on the length of the novel. One *Life* article included a photograph of Jones staggering under the weight of the novel, which had run to over twelve hundred printed pages.

Some Came Running needed more editorial work from Scribner's than it received. Jones (and perhaps Lowney) was responsible for the lack of editorial scrutiny and the failure to tighten scenes. Burroughs Mitchell and his wife, Helen, had visited the colony when the novel was nearing completion, and Helen remarked that the manuscript would need some revision. Mitchell told his wife, "You talk too much." Jones angrily wrote Mitchell on July 23, 1956, that a few minor cuts might be needed but that "you yourself told me in so many words that it needed no revision, major or minor" (MacShane 148). *Eternity* had made vast sums for Scribner's, and Mitchell, not wanting to alienate his best-selling author, backed away from doing editorial work that would have improved the novel.

Throughout the last stages of completing the novel, Jim was emotionally distressed and had experienced several attacks of nerves. He knew that the "barbs and hooks and knives and harpoons" of the literary people were "being sharpened" (MacShane 147). Photographs of Lowney taken at the time indicate she also was under great stress. She appears gaunt and distraught. She looks more than a generation older than Jim.

7

Colonists Get Published and Jim Leaves for New York

Norman Mailer and Jim Jones were friends for a time. Mailer talked about his early reaction to *Eternity* in the PBS documentary *James Jones: Reveille to Taps*, later published in the *Paris Review*: "It knocked me down and half knocked me out. I thought it was an extraordinary book. All the while I was reading it I had a sinking feeling, 'Well, you're no longer the most talented writer to come out of World War II. You've been replaced.' Extraordinary sensation. I've always felt I understood kings losing their crowns ever since" (Lennon 212).

The Mailer-Jones friendship flourished for several years before it began to break down, partly because of stories spread by a colonist, Jerry Tschappat, who published under the name Gerald Tesch. The problems apparently began after Scribner's turned Jerry's book down and he then placed it with Putnam's. Tschappat was angry and struck out at Lowney and Jim. According to Jim's letter to Mailer of March 5, 1956, Jerry had been writing to acquaintances about Jim and Lowney: "and I expect it was pretty lurid—how we kicked him out, destroyed his soul, kept him from getting his book published, etc.—also what a drunk I am and what a tyrant Lowney is" (*To Reach Eternity* 234–35). Jim believed that friends and publishers in New York were then spreading these stories being planted by Jerry.[1]

Jerry was reporting that Norman and others "were planning yourselves a secret little conspiracy to get Jones away and out from under the domination of that fearful woman Lowney Handy" (236). With grim humor Jim wrote to Norman: "let me remind you that while all you boys may have great will power and strength of character, I do not, and I need somebody to look after me and keep me from killing myself drinking and fucking, somebody who has some common sense, like Lowney, and also I need somebody to read over my stuff and tell me if it is good or not. Because I never know, like you and Vance [Bourjaily] and [James] Purdy do" (237–38).

Mailer then sent Jerry Tschappat a letter, dated March 24, 1956, saying he did not want to hear stories about Jones and Lowney. He sent a copy of his letter to Jim. Jim responded to Mailer on March 31, 1956, in a fairly friendly way, but spent much of the letter trying to set the record straight about Jerry. According to Jim, Jerry had been at the colony five times, and Lowney had run him off four times. "One of those times," Jim wrote, "Lowney went to work on him with her fists and knocked him around a bit, and the last time she ran him off told him he had graduated; he could never come back." Jim went on to say that the "humanity-loving, proletarian-loving, rights of man-loving" Mailer probably could not understand Lowney's violent behavior and her letting Jerry return several times. Jim enumerated Jerry's troublemaking: He "had gotten so cocky nobody could talk to him, and also . . . he had been tempting me deliberately . . . to knock the shit out of him, something which I am glad to say I refrained from, because that was what he wanted, and would have enjoyed it too much, gotten too good an orgasm out of it" (*To Reach Eternity* 240).

In this long letter, Jim told Norman that Jerry's novel, *Never the Same Again*, had been potentially great, but that Jerry had resisted, in fact refused, Lowney's best advice. In Jerry's draft of his novel, the older man, Roy, seduced the young boy, Johnny. Lowney wanted Jerry to pull a switch—to have the boy seduce the man. Jim insisted that Lowney was right and that she was trying to make Jerry into a "really great writer" by facing himself. Jim did not think Jerry would ever make that introspective leap and would remain a "pathological liar." Jim admitted that he, too, had been given to lying in the past and still did "a lot of the time. But Im growing out of it a little, very painfully" (244).

Did Lowney deliberately scuttle Jerry's novel at Scribner's? Undoubtedly not, for she was eternally optimistic about the artistic potential of "the boys" (as she called them) in the Handy Colony. Jim was publishing short stories after *From Here to Eternity* had made him a hot property, and Lowney wanted to prove *Eternity* had not been a fluke. Several other "boys" finished novels that were rejected, or they fled the colony before they could complete their work. Lowney came up with fanciful explanations for the failures, but the world throughout 1955 could see that her students—except for Jim—had not found publishers.

In 1956, however, there was a breakthrough. Jerry Tschappat, using the pseudonym Gerald Tesch, published *Never the Same Again*. In addition, Lowney knew that Tom Chamales's *Never So Few* and Edwin Daly's *Some Must Watch* would appear the following year.

Lowney in conversation often railed against "queers" and did not want her boys reading or copying Proust. She did, however, oversee Tschappat's homosexual novel about an older man's seduction of a thirteen-year-old. George Adelman's review in the *Library Journal* for November 15, 1956, indicated why the novel was to have few sales:

> This very powerful first novel has much to recommend it but regrettably also has objectionable aspects that would preclude its being wanted by most public libraries. . . . Subject matter of this sort requires a masterful touch to avoid on the one hand, bad taste and sensationalism and on the other, mawkishness and morbidity. Remarkably enough the youthful author does have this masterful touch. His treatment of the confused boy and the lonely invert is Gide-like in its perceptiveness and sensitivity. However[,] and unfortunately it is a big however, Tesch has seen fit to pepper his work with vulgarisms and lurid passages, no doubt in the interests of verisimilitude. He has succeeded only in degrading what could otherwise have been an outstanding artistic achievement. (2693)

This review suggests that the novel might have succeeded in the 1990s, after gay literature had become commercially successful and language restraints had been lifted.

In a November 12, 1956, article headed "Housemother Knows Best," *Time* was particularly damning of the second published novel to have been written under Lowney's direction: "Tesch borrows from Jones the neo-Dreiserian conviction that life itself is a four-letter word. Among Tesch's victims and vermin: a girl who commits incest and goes mad, a wife-beating lush, an aging sadistic homosexual. The most defenseless victim is the English language, e.g., 'A pang of lonesomeness settled over him like a cold wet spray.' Some might argue that Tesch was a born bad writer. But Gerald, an off-and-on Handy colonist since 1952, has apparently been trained to write this way" (127).

In an article in the *Chicago Sunday Tribune Magazine* of July 14, 1957, entitled "She Teaches Tough Guys to Write," clearly written from Lowney's interviews, Tesch (then twenty-four) was said to have had no formal schooling after the sixth grade. According to the reviewer, William Leonard, the novel "was studiously avoided by book reviewers, received little exploitation, sold few copies, but still excites some interest in certain literary circles." Tesch was reportedly nearing the end of his second novel, "Alley Titanic," but it was never published (19).

Lowney was not one to take satisfaction in Jerry's poor sales and bad reviews. He was a colonist in 1956, was away in 1957, and back in residence in 1958. Lowney almost always forgave those she chased away, even if she had used violence to run them off, and Jerry proved no exception to this rule.

Edwin "Sonny" Daly, from Marshall, began working with Lowney on a novel while he was still in high school. He did not, however, live on the colony grounds. Daly told Steve Kash, in an interview published in the *Terre Haute Tribune Star* in 1998: "Lowney was very dynamic and supportive. She would help if you worked, but she had no tolerance for people who were lazy" (Kash 10). Lowney had seen great promise in Daly, but she could not have been pleased with the notices of his novel. Oliver La Farge began his review in the *Saturday Review* for March 23, 1957: "For a youth to start a novel like *Some Must Watch* . . . at sixteen and finish it at nineteen was so remarkable that, like Johnson's dog walking on its hind legs, one is inclined to ignore whether it is well done. This is exceptional work for so young a writer and it earns Edwin Daly that good old label 'promising.' Much of the actual writing, I gather, was done at the Handy Colony for young writers. I do hope that before he goes much further, Edwin Daly may be exposed to experienced criticism and above all to someone with an ear for the English Language" (12–13).

David Ray, the renegade colonist who wrote about the deficiencies of Lowney's teaching method and the horrors of her summer camp, weighed in with a putdown in the *New Republic* for April 22, 1957: "Daly, whom James Jones describes on the cover of *Some Must Watch*, as an American answer to Francoise Sagan, portrays what the publisher describes as 'a way of life typically American . . . the American boy.' The volume is not offered as a juvenile, and so the reader looks for some central concern or meaning in it. It isn't there" ("Mrs. Handy's Recipes" 19–20).

In the summer of 1957, William Leonard in the July 14 *Chicago Sunday Tribune Magazine*, noted that Daly's novel was "an acutely telling scrutiny of a deteriorated parent-son relationship." Daly's father was no longer speaking to Lowney. "'What's he sulking about?' Lowney asks. 'Sonny put him on the map'" (19). However much Lowney relished the role of town gadfly, the unfavorable notices of Daly's novel were a blow to her.

Lowney was more successful with Tom Chamales's *Never So Few*, which was awarded both critical and financial success. Maxwell Geismar in the *Saturday Review* for March 23, 1957, called it "an extraordinary first novel of the Burma guerillas—the Kachin tribesmen with their American and English leaders—during the Second World War. It is an exotic and absorbing experience that one lives through in the dense pages of this book, full of pain, suffering, and death." Although Geismar had minor reservations about the novel, he found the story of life with the Kachins behind the Japanese lines in Burma "brilliant" (12).

R. A. Hoey in the *Library Journal* for March 15, 1957, picked up the theosophical and mystical elements in the novel: "Pervaded with a 'razor's edge' sort of mystic philosophy, even the language and sex scenes, though strictly G.I., seem to give stature to the whole" (749). Maugham's *The Razor's Edge* was a favorite work of Lowney's, and she undoubtedly had Tom reading it. Tom was drawn to mystical and occult ideas as few of Lowney's students were, and this was a special bond between the two. Lowney and Tom worked together closely, they were a team as close as Fred Astaire and Ginger Rogers, and they were able to get philosophical and mystical ideas into his novels without slowing the action or making characters into cardboard spokespersons for those ideas.

Reviewers did see the strength and power of the work. The influential *Kirkus* review January 15, 1957, obviously pleased Lowney: "This stands out of the welter of novels told against the background of war for its originality and distinction. Much of it is unpalatable, raw, distasteful, assuredly not for the thin skinned. But the impact is terrific, and the whole picture of the guerilla fighting in Burma emerges with its strange undertones of intense patriotism, its moments of almost spiritual aspiration, its violence and crudity" (45).

Lowney considered Chamales in the same league as Jim, both artistically and financially. She often bragged that the film rights for Tom's first novel were sold for three hundred thousand dollars, almost four times the sum fetched by *From Here to Eternity*. Chamales's success buoyed her spirits temporarily, but through much of 1956 there was a problem with Jim's unfinished second novel.

Jim was living in his new and expensive house on the edge of the colony grounds, but he was not far enough away to be shielded from Lowney's erratic ways—her nerves were bad in 1956 and the barbiturates she took did little to calm her. There were problems with colony administration at times, for some colonists disliked her authoritarian ways. Harry's role at the colony was not well understood by the colonists. Lowney's forceful personality overshadowed his accomplishments as mediator. His financial support was too often taken for granted. Many years after Don left the colony, he sent Harry a box of tree-ripened mangoes. Lowney wrote that Harry was touched by Don's thoughtfulness, and she added that not many people "remembered" Harry. Lowney constantly looked for support from Harry and knew he should not have been forgotten.

Jim, under pressure to complete a second novel, knowing that many critics were likely to savage his next work of fiction, had worked himself into exhaustion. According to an article in *Life*, February 11, 1957, "The Good Life of James Jones," he wrote every day of the week, including Saturday and Sunday, beginning at 5:30 A.M. and writing until noon, then he relaxed with his "toys": rifles, pistols, pipes, Meissen figures, toy soldiers, bowie knives, and chess sets. He read in his large library and ran two miles each day—the running was a "spiritual thing" (Hoey 83).

During the years he had been writing *Some Came Running*, he had contributed heavily to the Handy Colony (Lowney requested that her students to give her 10 percent of their royalties). Jim gave her and the colony more than 10 percent of his earnings from *Eternity* and had gone in debt for his expensive house. Lowney told the *Newsweek* reporter Robert E. Cantwell, in an article titled "James Jones: 'Another Eternity'?" published November 23, 1953, that Jim had already spent from sixty to a hundred thousand dollars on the colony, was paying for the new house and the land around it, and was continuing to spend heavily on the colony. Lowney said he was going to be kept busy for the next few years (103). What was implicit in Lowney's comments was that she had economic control over him. Her prediction was almost true, but her hold over him was eventually to fail.

Don Sackrider, then a copilot with Eastern Airlines, paid a surprise visit to Lowney and Jim in November 1956. This was the first time he had seen them since the summer of 1953 when Lowney kicked him out of the colony. The visit was cordial, and Don saw no hint of trouble between Lowney and Jim as they gave him a tour of Jim's house. Jim proudly showed him the manuscript of *Some Came Running*, stacked on top of a radiator. Jim measured it in inches, like snowfall: two feet. This was the first time Don had met Jim and Lowney on an equal footing, as an adult. He was twenty-seven then, and he now believes that Jim's seeing Don free and happy and successful on his own may have had a subtle effect on Jim's subsequent breaking away. Jim hid his psychological stress from Don; he was on tranquilizers and gin late in 1956 as he was completing *Some Came Running* (MacShane 148). Jim needed to escape from the problems brought on by Lowney's increasingly frequent emotional scenes, as she coped with his unhappiness in the controlled environment of Marshall and the Handy Colony.

Lowney had predicted to Don in 1947 that Jim would eventually leave her and marry. At times both Lowney and Jim knew they would eventually part. Don was with Lowney and Jim when they saw the movie *All About Eve* when it was released in 1950. It was obvious to Don that both Jim and Lowney immediately saw the implications of the older woman and her relationship with the younger man, a relationship being played out in real life by the two stars, Bette Davis and Gary Merrill. For years Lowney and Jim had known about Thomas Wolfe's personal life—how Wolfe had been aided by the older woman Aline Bernstein and how he had broken with her and then savaged her in his fiction (as Jones was eventually to do in his fictional presentation of Lowney in *Go to the Widow-Maker*).

Although Lowney knew that Jim would eventually leave her, she did not let him go easily. In her jealousy she spied on him. When Don was at the colony he needed some dental work done, and Lowney arranged for him to go with Jim to St. Louis to see a dentist there. What Lowney wanted to find out, Don remembers, was "what kind of trouble Jim was getting into" when he was away from Marshall. Jim and Don did go to a cocktail party, and upon their return Lowney questioned Don closely about the trip and the people Jim met.

There was also the fear of incest. Lowney and Jim had portrayed themselves to the public as surrogate mother and son for such a long time that it seemed to seep into a part of their own visualizations of themselves. After the Lowney-Jim breakup, Jim saw their relationship in a new way. In *Go to the Widow-Maker* he fictionalized these incestuous fears. In that novel, he wrote, "As Carol Abernathy [Lowney] in one of her better moments once chuckled and said huskily as they lay in bed, 'Christ! You're the only man I ever heard of who got to live out his Oedipus complex!' Grant [Jones] had laughed, at the time" (160).

Jim was also under great emotional strain as he was completing his complex novel, for he feared that his second novel would not be a blockbuster as *Eternity* had been. He needed to talk to his editors about the manuscript, and in December 1956 he left Marshall for New York.

8
Jim's Marriage and Its
Consequences for the Colony

On his first day in New York, Jones met Budd Schulberg and stayed with him in his apartment for a time. Schulberg recalled that Jim "seemed at loose ends—somewhere between breaking away from his life in Illinois and not knowing exactly where he could break to." Jim told his new friend that he needed a woman, and he described what he was look-ing for: "I'd like someone who looks something like Marilyn Monroe for openers, but who is intelligent, knows writers, who's interested in writing, with a great sense of humor." Schulberg knew just the right woman for Jim—his former girlfriend and friend, Gloria Mosolino, a beautiful blonde who had been a stand-in for Marilyn Monroe, had written an unpublished novel, and knew many writers (Lennon 219–20). Gloria (called Moss by her friends) described herself to Willie Morris as a "writer fucker" (*James Jones* 87). When Schulberg called Gloria to arrange a blind date, he told her she would like Jim. In fact, he predicted, "I think you're going to marry him" (Lennon 219–20).

Their first date began inauspiciously. He was two hours late and drunk. He was drunk on their second date, too, but Gloria remarked, "I kind of like him." After the third date, she said, "He drinks a lot, but he's fun and I'm in love and I'm going to marry him" (MacShane 151).

Lowney learned of Jim's love affair in New York. She told Don Sackrider many years later that she sent Jim a telegram advising him to get married. Her recollection was correct. She wrote Harry on March 3, 1957, just a few days after Jim and Gloria's wedding, that she had tried to phone Jim in New York but he would not take her call. She then sent him this wire: "APRIL IS A BEAUTIFUL MONTH TO BE MARRIED IN . . . CONGRATULATIONS AND BEST WISHES" (UIS). Lowney's peaceful acceptance of Jim's plans to marry did not last long, however.

Gloria was young, beautiful, uninhibited, and a comedienne — absolutely different from Lowney. Jim and Gloria began to talk of marriage. Jim returned to Marshall and immediately invited Gloria to join him. Lowney was away in Florida at the time, and the two young lovers had several days together. Then they drove to Florida. Jim did not tell Gloria about his long relationship with Lowney. For years he had kept up the public pretense that Lowney was his godmother or his adopted mother, though the colonists and residents of Robinson knew, or at least suspected, otherwise. Jim stuck to the public story, but he did not allow the two women to meet and soon sent Gloria back to New York. Jim then spoke to Lowney, who was long accustomed to handling him. She thought that Gloria was just a gold digger and that she was likely to leave him and win large alimony payments. Lowney suggested that Jim insist on a prenuptial agreement. When Jim suggested such an agreement to Gloria she refused, for she intended to stay married to the man she wed. Jim phoned her back, saying, "I think you had better come down here" (Mac-Shane 154). Gloria joined Jim in Florida, where, Tom Chamales reported to Lowney, they all partied. Jim and Gloria then left for Haiti, where they were to be married.

Ever mercurial, Lowney now had no plans to let Jim marry. "I have figured out how to stop Jamie-boy," she wrote Harry. She was going to turn the colony over to Jim and Tom Chamales, apparently believing that Jim would immediately give up his plans to marry Gloria (February 21, 1957, UIS).

She wrote the agent, Ned Brown, that same day that she was ill, had been told by her doctor to live quietly, and was giving up her work with students. She said of Jim, "he's a frightened, perplexed and angry little boy. He goes to New York and everyone makes over him, he comes back home with a head the size of the Empire State Building." Lowney tried to make it clear what her intentions were: "WHAT I WANT TO DO IS PROTECT JIM'S NAME FOR POSTER-ITY."[1] She explained:

> Everytime Jim goes to New York he comes home so full of hatred and anger at me he sits in the same room, and the waves of feeling are as strong as if he were beating me with his fists. This usually doesn't last too long. He goes to New York, gets frightened, or gets off the beam from too much adulation (THIS IS WHAT DESTROYS ALL YOUR BEST ACTORS . . .

VANITY) and the girls — they all get him to thinking that he is mistreated, dominated by this awful old elderly lady. [H]e makes them think I won't let him have any dates. . . . He gets women to feeling sorry for him. They think he's almost a virgin, hasn't seen a woman for three years because I don't allow it. Most of them think I force him to sleep with me at the point of a gun . . . or a refusal to help him in his work if he dont. He tells all of them he will marry them . . . and then says he asks me because he has to have my help. Then he tells them I won't let him.

Lowney was in an agitated state after Jim had told her he wanted to marry Gloria:

this Mosoline. He's promised her to marry her. He told her he had to come and see me and get my permission. He also told her I was 59 years old [she was fifty-three] and horrible looking, when she asked him if I had slept with him. Then he comes here, and moves into my apartment, and then told all over Hollywood [Florida] WHERE I HAVE BEEN COMING FOR YEARS that he wanted to get married but I won't let him. . . . He hasn't written the girl or called her since he came, and at present (or last Sunday) he and Tom [Chamales] talked to me from Palm Beach and Jim told me that the girls were thick as flies. . . . I had asked Tom to set up a real SETUP for him and keep him occupied until I get rested and back on my feet.

Lowney then revealed more about her precarious psychological state: The night that Tom came to take Jim to Palm Beach, she "had threatened to call police twice and have him thrown out of my place, scandal or no scandal and I was in a complete collapse." Instead of elaborating on her collapse she wrote a long section about Jim's diving instructor "mixed up with the rackets who rolled [Jim] for $2000 in less than a week." Apparently Lowney confronted this three-hundred-pound diving teacher, he threatened to hit her, and she pulled a knife on him. Her description is chilling in light of her attack on Gloria, with a knife, later that year:

I put the fear of God in that guy's heart because I'd just as soon killed him as not and I come of killing people. My father's people were all killers. Uncle John Turner (second chapter of FROM HERE TO ETERNITY) was my father's youngest brother [who would] as soon kill you as look at you. Dad's father shot and killed three men in front of his home in Kentucky, and wounded the fourth, who crawled off up the holler — four men against one — and he came clear in the trial. So don't think I wouldn't have put that EX-NEW YORK COP — exCoastGuard sonofabitch out of his misery. I told him I only had a year to live and there was nothing I'd like better than to take him with me, and do his wife a favor. (February 21, 1957, UIS)

Jim recycled in fictional form some of this material about Al Bonham, the instructor, in *Go to the Widow-Maker*.

In the same letter, Lowney wrote Ned that she was beginning to think Jim should "marry that gal in N.Y. Scandal or no scandal." Harry thought Lowney should go to Haiti with Jim, for Lowney and Harry both believed Jim's relationship with the diving instructor was a mistake and Lowney could keep Jim from getting "tied up with some other jerk." Lowney then thought he could go without her and get into trouble, for "THIS IS WHERE HIS BOOKS COME FROM."

Jim went to Haiti, but he took Gloria, not Lowney. They checked into the Hotel Oloffson, where Betty Comden (famous member of the Broadway songwriting team Comden and Green) and her husband, Steve Kyle, along with Dr. Ben Wolstein (a psychiatrist) and his wife were among those in residence. These two couples and Gloria and Jim were congenial, and they had a few relaxing days. As Jim and Gloria's wedding day approached, though, the atmosphere changed. Gloria was concerned about the rowdiness she observed among Jim and his friends during several parties in Florida before the two of them left for Haiti. She was in "emotional turmoil." Among other things she suspected the nature of Jim's relationship with Lowney, but he continually denied it. On the day of the wedding, Jim and Dr. Wolstein spent several hours walking around the grounds of the Hotel Oloffson. Jim also had doubts. He felt guilty: "He had been unfaithful to Lowney; would he be the same to Gloria? Was he suited to any extended personal relationship?" (MacShane 155). Lowney's and Harry's emotions were also stormy. Lowney was in near collapse because of the impending loss of her star student and lover. Jim for years had been a major financial supporter of the colony.

Jim and Gloria were married on February 27, 1957. The Wolsteins and Betty Comden and her husband were present for the ceremony. Tom Chamales, in Miami, was broke and tried to borrow money from Lowney for the trip. She refused, and he found another lender. He arrived the day after Jim and Gloria were married. The Wolsteins and Chamales appear in fictional form in Jones's Go to the Widow-Maker. Chamales is presented in an unfavorable light. It seems he was feeding Lowney gossip about Jim and Gloria at the same time he was posing as their friend, and Jim must have learned his friend could not be trusted.

At first, Lowney wanted it known that Jim's marriage was for the best. She wrote Harry on March 3, 1957, that she was going to get back to her own writing; she had a play in mind. She had grown tired of being Jim's servant—"cooking, working until I was sick—he getting the credit—or 90% of the cash—and more and more he resented working with me as I did with him. We were always battling, silently or violently verbally." She wanted to take credit for pushing him into marriage, for she had sent him that telegram: "APRIL IS A BEAUTIFUL MONTH TO BE MARRIED IN." Lowney had her own interpretation of the effects of that message: "The girl knew he was mad and tried and tried to see the wire, and when he finally got drunk enough he showed it—and she took him to task for letting me dominate him—and he not acting like a man. She got the idea of marriage from the wire—and went to work." Lowney asserted that she pushed Jim into marriage because he had earlier told one of the Handy colonists that he would marry to spite Lowney. Although Lowney had been in a state of near collapse after Jim had told her about Gloria, she told Harry, "I figured I'd help him into it [marriage]" (UIS).

Lowney insisted to Harry (incorrectly) that the marriage with Gloria was not legal in the United States: "NAPOLEONIC CODE." She had an idea, though, "that the gal will keep him. And good riddance."

Lowney thought she knew the couple's motives: "He . . . thought he would get a lot of publicity—and the gal thinks she is going to get in the movies—but I've stopped that. Jim is going to find out he's been a fool—and I hope the girl has to live in Marshall for a year. She'll learn a lot and so will he. I'm going to live easy."

At times in the letter to Harry, Lowney let her bitterness show. Jim had sold out his two best friends "for some pretty cheap crap." Five paragraphs later she declared that Jim was lonely and sad, not knowing how he had gotten into such trouble. She tried to reassure Harry she was happy with things as they were: "I'm tired of Jones getting the nasty stories about me in papers that he does—and all the people in New York that he tells about my dominating him. He'll not get a chance. Because I'm out of it completely—and from now on we'll see how well he writes on his own. He will have to crawl all the way back for me to ever work with him again—and do some growing up besides. I don't think it's in the books. I THINK I'VE GOT OTHER WORK CUT OUT FOR ME."

Lowney had a history of running colonists off after she had making a scene and saying rash things—and then allowing them to return as if nothing had ever happened. Of course, no other colonist had occupied such a place in her life as her Jamie had. Lowney ended her letter to Harry seemingly in a state of yogic bliss, accepting the changes in a mystical way: "Best love—didn't worry—it's all DIVINE WILL—and I know that I am going along a new path. So are you—and so is Jim—it's all in God's books. Jim was just too young to stand all the pressure—we had to get some of it off—he was too much of a legend—he was becoming to believe it himself." Lowney refused to believe that Jim was in love with Gloria.

Lowney did her best to blacken the reputation of Jim and Gloria. She wrote Horace Manges, legal adviser for Scribner's and a longtime friend of Jim's, on March 4, 1957, that Jim's creditors were getting concerned. He owed eight thousand dollars to the Marshall bank, had a twenty-five-thousand-dollar mortgage on his house, owed for the lot across the street from his house. She wanted Horace to work out a plan to give Jim a monthly sum only: "In this way, he would know that the woman who lived with him was not doing so for his money" (UIS).

Lowney was virtually out of control in her vicious attacks on Jim, Gloria, Budd Schulberg, and Ed Townsend (the diving instructor), and she kept referring to Ed's rolling Jim for big bucks, this letter indicating three thousand dollars instead of two thousand. She accused Jim of stealing books from her library. Gloria, she insisted, was a schemer: "Tom told me the Gal was a nice enough person, but that she didn't bat in our league. But it took me over three years to hook my husband, and I am wondering if she don't bat in a higher league than ours, since she landed James Jones in only three weeks."

Lowney told Horace that her doctor warned her she was "headed for a breakdown." She called on his sympathy by saying she had been bedridden for the past six weeks. "UNDER NO CIRCUMSTANCES," she wrote Manges, "do I intend to play mother-in-law to James Jones and this gal, who has been moving heaven and earth to get to meet me. I shall move completely out of the picture and let them work it out." Lowney had mulled over her belief that the couple's marriage was not legal in the United States. She put Jim in the worst possible light: "But knowing Jim as I do, he would be more liable to stick to a gal if it wasn't legal—put her on the spot—he has a sardonic sense of humor—he'd make her sweat and humiliate her—and they'll celebrate their Golden wedding anniversary" (UIS).

On March 5, Lowney wrote Harry again, and this time she was more bitter still. She referred to Jim's bride as Gloria Vanderbilt Mussolini. Her ethnic and religious biases surfaced: "BOTH TOM CHAMALES AND BUDD SCHULBERG have been very successful in pushing Jim into something. . . . When you got a Jew leading you—and a Greek shoving you—boy, you've been places" (UIS). Don believes her so-called racial slurs were just hot air. Lowney was always building up—even romanticizing—her father's friend Squab Wilson, the barber, the only black man in Marshall. All Marshall men went to Squab's shop for a haircut and for the news. Lowney told Don that Squab and his brother had tried to attend the University of Illinois. When they were rejected she sat on the steps and cried (Sackrider narrative).

Lowney wanted Harry to tell people in Robinson and Marshall about Jim and Gloria and what a fiasco this marriage was going to be. Jim's friends would be giving him a horselaugh, and that would be good for Jim, she asserted: "He needed to have a little air let out of that Empire-Building-Sized-head" (March 5, 1957, UIS). Lowney was certain that Jim could not write another book without her.

Tinks and Helen Howe drove up from their home in Robinson to the colony after Jim and Gloria's wedding. Tinks remembers, "Lowney was completely heartbroken. . . . You could tell she was completely broken. She tried to act like she wasn't but she really was. She didn't want Jim to get married." Helen remembers that visit: "She was tremendously sad. She was sorry that Jim's life no longer was in any way linked with hers. She was not ready to admit that she could not help him any further. But . . . Lowney was a tremendously strong woman. I don't think Lowney really thought he wouldn't be back. Because of the intensity of their relationship, and also because of what they gave to one another" (Lennon 220, 222).

In the midst of her tirades, Lowney did turn to a subject that had been a concern to her for a long time: Hemingway and masculinity. She wrote Ned Brown that a senior editor at Scribner's told Jim during the trip when he met Gloria that Lowney had made a man of Jim. "Now what is a man," Lowney pondered. She had not tried to make Jim a man: "I tried to make writers out of all my students." The editor's remark led her to her long-felt views about Hemingway: he "castrated his writing trying to prove he was a sportsman, and therefore, a man. Who in the hell cares if he killed a lion, or a bar [bear], or rode a rhinoceros across the full width of Africa" (February 21, 1957, UIS). Jim had been hearing similar remarks from Lowney for a long time, and in *Go to the Widow-Maker* he engaged the cult of masculinity in more sophisticated ways, but he reached a conclusion similar to Lowney's.

Jim and Gloria remained in Haiti for three months after their marriage. Finally they returned to Miami, drove to New York, and stayed there for a short time. Instead of making a clean break with Lowney, Jim decided that he and Gloria would return to his home in Marshall.

So Lowney now met the beautiful Gloria for the first time. At first Lowney was cordial, but she had been angry and frustrated for months at losing her Jamie. She told Gloria she could not use the swimming pool on the colony grounds, for Gloria in a bathing suit would excite the colonists sexually. Then Lowney began throwing out of her cabin all the belongings that Jim had left there. Gloria could hardly fail to recognize that Jim and Lowney had been lovers, but Jim continued to deny it.

Isolated from friends and family in a hostile environment, Gloria invited guests for the Fourth of July holidays—her young niece Kate Mosolino; Addie Herder, the painter; and Monique Gonthier, a designer. One afternoon while Gloria and her niece were in the vast living room of Jim's house, Gloria heard a loud noise. Lowney had burst through the back door, bowie knife in hand. "The only reason Jim married you," she screamed, "is that you're the best cocksucker in New York."

Gloria managed to get her niece out of the room before Lowney lunged at her. The two women fell to the floor fighting. Jim came in to pull the two apart (MacShane 155–56).

What were Lowney's intentions? She often spoke of coming from a violent Kentucky family, from "killing people." Still, she may not have planned to kill or severely injure Gloria. She took Gloria by surprise and could easily have stabbed the younger woman. In her distraught state, Lowney may have thought the attack would be enough to scare Gloria away from Marshall, leaving Jamie for Lowney's ministrations. Or perhaps she had decided to get

Gloria and Jim out of her life entirely, and she used the attack as a way to run them off.

Whatever Lowney's intentions, Jim and Gloria left Marshall the next day, never to return. For the first time, Jim told Gloria that Lowney had been his mistress, and that he had slept with Lowney in Florida after he had proposed to Gloria. He tried to explain how Lowney had helped him for many years and why he was indebted to her. Gloria was particularly distressed because Jim had not been honest about his relationship with Lowney, had lied about it for months. Jim had prided himself on his truth-telling in life and in fiction; Gloria had trusted him; he had lied to her. The two drove aimlessly, fighting all the while. Gloria at times would get out of the car and walk before reentering the car. This struggle went on for several days, and finally the two began to resolve the issue that was tearing the marriage apart. One subject was forbidden: "If you bring [Lowney] up again," Jim said, "I'll just leave" (MacShane 157). They made their peace. Jim's past with Lowney was off-limits, and they could begin their life anew, first in New York, then in London, then in Paris, and finally in the United States once again. Years later, Jim wrote about Lowney and the break with her in *Go to the Widow-Maker*.

In New York, Jim and Gloria moved among writers, artists, and show people—a social life Lowney had tried to keep Jim away from—and it was an exhilarating time for both of them. He saw *Some Came Running* through the press and endured with grace its ferocious reviews. It was soon filmed, starring Frank Sinatra, Shirley Maclaine, and Dean Martin. Jim set to work on a short novel, *The Pistol* (1959), which was written quickly and demonstrated for the world to see that he could write without Lowney's editorial help. A superbly crafted symbolic novella, it was very different from the two sprawling novels he had written under Lowney's influence.

After the Joneses moved to Paris in 1958, Jim wrote *The Thin Red Line* (1963), the second novel of his army trilogy, and perhaps his greatest artistic success. Romain Gary wrote Jim that the novel was "a realistic fable, symbolic without symbols, mythological and yet completely factual, a sort of Moby Dick without the white whale, deeply philosophical without any philosophizing whatsoever. The book belongs to that vein of poetic realism which is the rarest and to me most precious thing in the whole history of the novel; it is essentially an epic love poem about the human predicament and like all great books it leaves one with a feeling of wonder and hope" (MacShane 203).

Four years later, Jim published *Go to the Widow-Maker*, an openly autobiographic novel that deals fictionally with Jim's meeting Gloria and their love affair, the break with Lowney and Lowney's attack on Gloria, Gloria's distress at being lied to by her new husband, and the resolution to the marital problems that almost drove Jim and Gloria apart. Jim was too close to the passions of love and hate to shape his material. The novel is set in Jamaica and contains some of Jim's best writing. The underwater scenes, in particular, are dazzling. Jim's views concerning Lowney had hardened over the years, and Lowney's fictional self (Carol Abernathy) is shown harshly in the novel. Carol is a shrill old woman, provincial, demanding, hysterical, and emotionally troubled, without any talents of her own. The fictional Harry is written off in the novel as a hopeless alcoholic who will stand by his wife, no matter what she might do. Jim hated his Lowney-like character too much to humanize her.

This is the way Jim fictionalized Lowney's attack on Gloria. Grant (the fictional Jim) is in the shower and can hear voices in the kitchen, then "cocksucker" repeated and repeated. When he turns off the water, he hears the hysterical Carol shouting, "I don't give a damn! You'll not lock me out! I have as much right here as you have! More! Don't you *ever* try to lock me out! What did you ever do for him? Fuck him! That's all! He only married you because you were a good easy lay! The best cocksucker in New York! That's what he told me, Yes!" (*Go to the Widow-Maker* 458). By the time Grant is out of the shower and comes into the kitchen, Carol has broken through the screen door, "her mouth shouting as if it were a separate creature." Jim duplicated in fiction the actual scene in Marshall, with one omission: Carol is not pictured with a knife in her hand, as Lowney had appeared when she burst through the screen door into the house.

Jim put aside all the good qualities in Lowney and Harry when he fictionalized them. Tom Chamales is presented in an unfavorable light also: as an unreliable and violent schemer. Jim is not any easier on himself in portraying the Grant character, pathological in his distrust of his wife (Lucky) and her relationships with other men. Lucky is presented as a liberated woman, bright, beautiful, and seductive. Though she is slow to forgive Grant for lying to her about his long affair with Carol, she eventually does. The fictional presentations of Jim, Gloria, Tom, and several others are perceptively drawn, but Lowney and Harry are shown as only one-dimensional characters.[2]

Lowney is presented more favorably in colonist Jon Shirota's still unpublished and unproduced play, *The Last Retreat*. Shirota was the last student at the colony, and as such, he knew Lowney when she was old and in poor health, taking almost no students. He came to the colony soon after Harry died. He had read Jim's novels but had not met him, though Lowney often talked about him. In Shirota's four-character play, the names have been changed but a recognizable Jim and Lowney are the two main characters. The two students in residence at the colony are a war novelist, sleeping with the Lowney character, and a young black writer. Lowney is first seen meditating in her cabin on the colony grounds. Jim's mansion can be seen through the window. More subtly than Bowers, Shirota has captured the personality and language of his Lowney-like character.

Shirota envisions what might have been if the best-selling novelist's marriage had failed after ten years and he in an alcoholic stupor had come back to his mansion just outside the colony gate. He has written a subtle, sensitive play, humanizing all the characters. The Jim character is in despair, his last novel having been rejected. At the end Lowney puts aside — burns — her own novel in order to devote herself full-time to helping her former student-lover. Shirota's fantasy — what would have happened if Jim had returned to Lowney — is psychologically sound, but he was right in fictionalizing and renaming the two central characters. Jim and Gloria were married for life. Nothing — not even a force such as Lowney — could drive them apart.

9
The Final Years

The first months of 1957 were terrible ones for Lowney. Her Jamie was now married to a young and beautiful woman. She was unsure what to do with her own life. She seriously considered giving up the directing of the Handy Colony but wisely decided to keep busy with colony work. By early summer, Jim and Gloria were back in Marshall, their presence a constant reminder that Lowney had lost her Jamie. Her students had returned, but there were fewer of them that summer: seven men and two women whose names are not given (Wood and Keating, xl) were living in the trailers, not in the barracks. There were three major articles about the colony that year—some written before Lowney's attack on Gloria, some after that event—but all the accounts were favorable. In every article, Lowney seems to have controlled the interview, which suggests she was recovering from the loss of her lover.

A long article in the *Chicago Sunday Tribune* was obviously written before the July 4 holiday when Lowney attacked Gloria. In this article, titled "She Teaches Tough Guys to Write," William Leonard praises Lowney's methods of teaching and her success in placing the novels her "boys" had written. The article was particularly well illustrated. The half-page photograph of Lowney shows her looking old and tired. The small photograph on the first page shows Lowney in a more favorable light: For the photographer, she flashed her toothy smile, and she is gesturing, no doubt making a point about her successful authors. Gloria is looking fondly at Jim in their photograph. One colonist is shown working on the brick pile; another is shown outside, writing; another is shown at KP duty in the ramada; and two of the young men are shown outside their barracks building. The story reads: "Jim and his bride of four months, . . . who once was among other things a stand-in for Marilyn Monroe, live here with Gloria's cat, Charles, and Jim's collections of guns, knives, books, and recordings." *Mosolino*, however, was spelled *Mussolino*, no doubt reflecting Lowney's fine Italian hand. By the time the story appeared, Jim and Gloria were gone and could not request a correction.

Charles Wright and William Duhart

Two other major articles about the Handy Colony in 1957 concerned Charles Wright and William Duhart, young black novelists, and appeared in *Sepia* and *Ebony*. The articles were written and the photographs taken in the summer after Jim and Gloria had fled, but they were not published until late in the year.

Charlie Wright had come to the Handy Colony five years before. He had read about Lowney and the colony, no doubt in *Life*, and wrote to her. After some months of correspondence, Lowney asked him to join the group. When he arrived in Marshall, a small town with only one black man (the barber) in permanent residence, Wright decided to call Lowney to see if he was really welcome. Harry answered and said, "Of course; come out."

Wright's recollections of the first day he was there were included in an article entitled "Writer's Colony" in *Sepia*: "Lowney treated me real nice, but the second day she chewed me out for feeling sorry for myself. She has often told me she feels Negroes and Jews are their own worst enemy. 'We all give the enemy the gun to shoot us with,' is the way she puts it." Wright had served in the army in Korea and resisted Lowney's discipline. She kept running him off because he was not working and "couldn't stand the pressure Lowney puts on us" (36). At other times, he was afraid he was not cut out to be a writer.

Jim had to help him get haircuts. It is ironic that the black barber, Squab Wilson (a friend of Lowney's father), was afraid he would lose his white customers if he cut Wright's hair. Jim went to see Squab and told him the writers at the colony would boycott his shop if he persisted. The *Sepia* reporter concluded: "Under such a threat from one of the town's richest and most famous citizens, Wilson found himself with a new head of hair to cut" (38). Lowney claimed to run a colony free of racial and religious bigotry. "A man is a man," she told the *Sepia* reporter, "and that's all there is to it" (36).

When it came to evaluating leading black writers such as Richard Wright, Langston Hughes, Chester Himes, Ann Petry, Frank Yerby, and others, Lowney was opinionated and not always a shrewd critic: "I've read some of them," she said, "Hughes, of course, and Richard Wright. I think Richard Wright suffers from the actual, concrete things that harm a writer most: politics, women, drink, money and ambition. He has been ruined by an obsession with social harm and injustice, like Norman Mailer, and has become a pamphleteer" (40). Lowney seemed to have forgotten that she had encouraged many of her students to explore social issues in their novels.

Lowney then became even more specific in her evaluation of the direction black writers should take: "I have felt it would be best if they could learn to write about white people, just as I feel that women should learn to write about men, and that men should learn to write about women. All of which often is very hard for all concerned" (40). Suggesting that black writers learn to write about whites appears reasonable, but Lowney, it seems, had forgotten her advice to her students to look into themselves and write about what they knew. The two black writers there that summer knew the black world best.

Lowney probably gave Wright some other well-meaning but bad advice. He placed a first novel, *The Highest Tension*, with a publisher, but Lowney made him retract the manuscript for additional revisions. It was apparently never published.

William H. Duhart, the thirty-six-year-old black writer from Chicago who came to the Handy Colony from a Wisconsin prison, had some initial success. He was said by the *Sepia* reporter to have sold one paperback mystery novel, title not given, and was negotiating with Gold Medal Books to publish another mystery, *The Deadly Pay-Off*. The publisher did bring out the novel in 1958, but that was apparently Duhart's last publication. It was a better-than-average pulp story, with good control of underworld language. The main characters are white, however, and Duhart, perhaps following Lowney's advice to write about whites, missed a good chance to write a mystery novel with major black characters. In the *Sepia* article, Jim Jones praised Duhart as "a man to be reckoned with" (36), and Lowney planned to take him along in the winter of 1957–1958 to California to work with him more. Wright was planning to spend the winter months in New York.

An *Ebony* article for November 1957 entitled "Writers' Colony: Woman Who Trained James Jones Is Tutoring Two Negro Authors" is notable for the way Lowney is shown as a benefactress of blacks. The article began, "Among writers' camps scattered over America, few encourage the entry of down-and-outers and, so far as is known, none has produced a successful Negro author" (114). The Handy Colony was praised as the exception, and Charlie Wright and Bill Duhart were featured. The article is especially noteworthy because of the fine photographs of those two writers, of Lowney, and of the colony itself.

In 1958, Duhart and Wright were again in residence at the colony. Only one other person joined them that year. No longer having generous subsidies from Jim, Lowney had to depend on her own funds (mostly from 10 percent of royalties from books written at the colony, that is, if the authors chose to honor their agreement, as many did not) and the four hundred dollars a month that Harry provided. She did, however, work with seven people in 1958 through correspondence. The number of colonists actually in residence continued to dwindle. In 1959 there were two colonists in Marshall and no correspondence students.

Although there were fewer students, Lowney could view an increasing number of colonist publications. Chamales's *Never So Few* and Daly's *Some Must Watch* appeared in 1957. In 1958, Jones published *Some Came Running* and Duhart's *The Deadly Pay-Off* appeared.

Tom Chamales

Tom Chamales, one of Lowney's favorite students, stayed in her life. His *Never So Few* was made into a successful MGM movie starring Frank Sinatra and Gina Lollobrigida. Tom had quickly produced a second novel, *Go Naked in the World* (1959), set in Chicago after World War II and similar in subject matter to *Some Came Running*. Chamales drew on his Greek American heritage, and again he convincingly introduced mysticism into his story. Gene Baro in the *New York Herald Book Review,* January 31, 1960, called the "characters spaciously conceived and lucidly presented." Baro went on, "And the life of certain elements in the Greek-American community in Chicago forms an engrossing subject" (6). In 1961, *Go Naked in the World* was filmed by MGM, starring Gina Lollobrigida, Anthony Franciosa, and Ernest Borgnine.

Chamales's last months were difficult. He was deeply troubled psychologically and finally was confined for a time in a psychiatric facility. He was killed in a fire in 1960. Harry and Lowney attended his funeral in Chicago, Harry serving as a pallbearer. Before his death, he had attempted to begin a third novel. Lowney described that work and his emotional state in a letter to Charles Robb:

> About his third book. Tom came over to TUCSON and had about 3 pages on his book. He came twice—and I moved out of my room and gave him my typewriter and room and I slept on the davenport in the living room. BUT HE COULDN'T GET GOING. He had an awfully silly idea—writing about himself and Jones and two great successful guys going off to New York. It was awful. And he never wrote a line—came over twice and stayed about three weeks in all—and all but drove all of us batty. One night he awakened us lying at the front door—screaming let me out of here—he had had a lot of run-ins with police. (March 12, 1963, UIS)

In a rather confused paragraph, Lowney went on to say that after Tom's death a publisher announced a third Chamales novel, entitled "Forget I Ever Lived." Lowney was explicit in her comments: There was no third book. Still, Lowney cared deeply for Tom and helped him write two successful novels. Her distress when he was staying with her in Arizona had subsided, and she wandered into some statements about his enemies, the Jesuits whom she called "the INTERNATIONAL YID."

Jere Peacock

Jim and Chamales had had successes with their World War II novels, and Lowney thought Jere Peacock might be a winner, also. One of the two students at the colony in 1959, he was also in residence in 1960, 1961, and 1962, apparently alone, for the other student was Harry, who certainly spent much of his time in Robinson (Wood and Keating xxxix–xli). In 1960, Lowney did work with three students, including Peacock, in Tucson, where she was wintering. She also began correspondence with Jon Shirota, destined to be the last student in residence at the colony, and gave financial assistance to three students, including Willard Lindsay, who still had not been able to publish his novel.

Jere Peacock's *Valhalla* was reviewed favorably in the *New York Times Book Review* on January 8, 1961. David Dempsey began: "There are times in this novel when Jere Peacock, an ex-Marine, seems to be doing for post-war Japan what James Jones, an ex-dogface, did for pre-war Hawaii: immortalizing the immortality of the peacetime soldier. And there are times when he succeeds. This is a 'strong' novel that reeks of profanity, sex, and an explicit concern with the vulgar." Dempsey thought that Peacock was a serious writer, that it was not "a prurient book. Much of it is too dull for that; and all of it, as far as it goes, is true" ("Marines at Ease" 3).

Richard Gehman in the *Chicago Tribune Magazine of Books* for January 15, 1961, began with a devastating headline: "Blockbuster Lands: Greeted with a Yawn." The critic called it "a dull book, ill-conceived, torrentially written, dreadfully edited and overpriced." Gehman was convinced the book would have few readers "outside the author's immediate family and that strange circle in Marshall, Illinois den mothered by Ms. Lowney Handy, which gave us James Jones, Tom T. Chamales, and other members of the masculinity-is-meaning school" (3). Gehman's review is unduly harsh, and it is clear that he thought Peacock had suffered from his studying at the colony and working with Lowney. Peacock brought on some of his troubles with Gehman by thanking Lowney and Handy for their efforts as he was writing the book—for the Handy Colony had developed a bad reputation in many literary circles.

Peacock turned immediately to another novel, *To Drill and Die*, published in paper by Bantam in 1964. The theme is one explored in *From Here to Eternity*: the Individual versus the System. The novel, set in Korea, was ignored by reviewers. It is more controlled and focused than *Valhalla*, but the easygoing early 1960s was no time for a "saga of one man's fierce struggle to survive the brutally calculated efforts of the military to destroy him." The blurb writer for the back cover called it "a novel of staggering force that

124

takes its place beside *From Here to Eternity* as an expression of man's defiance and indomitable courage." *To Drill and Die* was dedicated to Harry, which undoubtedly pleased Lowney, for she knew how important Harry had been to the success of the colony. Too, Harry was sometimes in residence at the colony with Peacock while both were working on novels.

Peacock's second novel proved a disappointment to him and to Lowney, however. It appeared only in a paper edition and therefore was not reviewed. The novel showed that he continued to have a good ear for dialogue and a strong narrative drive. A quiet man, he was an acute observer of army life. He did not publish another novel. Perhaps he had written himself out, but more than likely he was discouraged by the reviewers' attacks on him for being one of Lowney's "boys."

Charles Robb

Charles Robb from Summit, New Jersey, without telling Lowney of his plans, had hitchhiked out to Robinson in the spring of 1953, hoping to gain admission to the colony. Harry and Lowney fortunately had just returned from Arizona. Robb had spent the first half of the year as a student at the University of Pennsylvania, but he left his studies to become a novelist. Robb was shy but determined. Lowney, of course, took him in. It was apparently not an easy time for either of them. He wrote her in an undated letter the year after his first session at the Handy Colony:

> I know that last summer I was terribly afraid of you because you could yell so loud. That was why I left early. I was getting to be nothing but a "yes" man and it was no good. A man is not made to back down to anybody. . . . Whether I come back or not is up to you. I don't expect you to be sweet-sweet with me like you were last year. But I am not sure that I am yet strong enough to carry on a war with you and win. I need more road work to get in condition. Please let me know whether you want me back or not. I will probably come anyway. . . . [He had spent the months after he left the colony living with his parents] because they would let me, mainly because they thought they had a chance of luring me back to college. It was tough for me to discipline myself in a house where everybody goes to bed at midnight and there is always liquor and a television set. But discipline is what it takes to be a writer. . . . [He was saying the right things to Lowney about discipline, and he went on to explain his struggles as a young writer] For the first three or four months of the winter I didn't write a word that was worth a shit. It was an awful feeling, like when your bowels lock and you need an enema. . . . I stuck it out and I'm glad. There was a day I saw a spark of hope, then a couple more weeks went by and I thought the spark had perished. But days when I felt a promise began to come more and more often. They are still coming irregularly—things will go swell for two or three days and then I'll ball it up somehow. (UIS)

Robb was working on a novel, *After Dinner Cenotaph*, and several short stories, during his 1955, 1956, and 1957 sessions at the colony. Drafts of his letters and creative work show that he was deliberate, almost obsessive, in his revisions. None of his prose was ever published. After he left the colony, he turned to keeping an extensive journal and to writing poetry. After Robb's death in 1997, the James Jones Literary Society in 1998 published his *Selected Poems*.

Robb was too shy to make many friends at the colony, but Charles Wright was an exception. They corresponded and met over the years, and in his will Robb left some money to Wright. It was because of his slowness in answering a request from Charles Wright that Lowney wrote him one of her caustic letters. In the early spring of 1963, the last year of the Handy Colony, Charles Wright was the only student in residence. While Charles was ill with flu, he wrote to Robb to send a manuscript Charles had left with him. Robb did not act quickly enough. So Lowney wrote Robb on April 15, 1963, that Charles had a bad case of the flu and her family in Marshall was looking after him, though he might need to go to the hospital. Her anger was everywhere to be seen in the letter: "WHY IN THE GOD DAMN HELL—DON'T YOU SEND THAT MATERIAL CHARLIE WROTE YOU ABOUT—you are a bum, or you'd have it here—he can use it when he gets well. . . . What an ass you are—YOU ARE ABOUT AS DUMB AS JIM JONES . . . and that is the ultimate I can think of."

Don Sackrider had seen Lowney many times in the winter of 1963–1964 and knew that she was being treated with barbiturates then. In the letter to Robb, she was out of control, spreading gossip about Budd Schulburg and Gloria Jones, with a constant refrain about "INTERNATIONAL YIDS." She accused Robb of being an intellectual and therefore one who would not write. She scrawled in the margin "You are so full of shit it runs out of your ears." She attacked him personally: "So you stick with the QUEERS AND THE NEW FRONTIER—and maybe you can go to lunch with Jackie [Kennedy]—or go to hell—BUT I'LL NEVER SEE YOU IN THIS LIFE—because you no longer are a writer—but a shit-head."

As if Lowney had not made her point in the typed text, she scrawled on the second page: "Get that material Charlie Wright ask[ed] you to send—get it here, so when he is well enough to work he has it and go fuck yourself. Lowney."

Robb then wrote his personal memo about this emotional letter Lowney had sent to him:

> I admit this letter and one from Charlie that came shortly after sure upset me and caused me to [do] the wrong thing: write letters back to them. Lowney has written "jealous" in one corner of the letter but doesn't say what I'm jealous about. My reaction is: "She thinks I'm jealous that she asked Charlie back to the Colony but not me." And I am. But at the same time I would not go back to the Colony for anything. Reading this letter over I feel as if Lowney is some*thing* (rather than some*one*) totally

beyond my understanding. Almost like some sea monster encountered on a dark night. Her unpredictable rages baffle me without arousing any curiosity to learn to understand them. She has become just another old crank as far as I'm concerned.

I guess another reason for my dismay over this letter and Charlie's was I had tried to do my best by them. Charlie had written a letter saying that after his arrival in Marshall he and Lowney had been through the mill. I had written back saying it takes two to quarrel and advising him to simply walk away from Lowney and ignore her when she started chewing him out.

I still think this is excellent advice. Also in the same letter I told Charlie not to answer my letter, that writers ought to write books not letters. It goes without saying that I have greatly weakened my position by immediately writing not one but two letters to both of them. Talk about making a fool of yourself.

Yet this is still what I believe.

What did I say wrong in my original letter? Perhaps really I didn't consider enough the effect I intended the letter to have. Nor did I give enough thought to the chance that Lowney might open the letter. I suppose the real mood of the letter was my usual: Let the chips fall where they may. If she can't see I mean well by her then fuck her. God knows I should feel happy Lowney asked Charlie back and that should be the end of it. God knows she did me a great favor in *getting him out of my hair.*

What interests me is women, and there are no appealing ones likely to be at the Colony.

It is just that I've had no success with women although I see handfuls of goodlooking ones every day that make me vulnerable to her ending: "So you stick with the QUEERS AND THE NEW FRONTIER—and maybe you can go to lunch with Jackie—or go to hell—BUT I'LL NEVER SEE YOU IN THIS LIFE etc."

And the "frustrations" Charlie spoke of in his letter. I am also experiencing these at this moment, mainly that I wrote those two letters after saying that about "writer should write books not letters." Doing that sure makes me hate myself. (Robb journal, UIS)

On September 25, 1984, Robb, in some notes about Jim, Lowney, and Harry, made it clear that the distress he felt after receiving Lowney's letter of April 15, 1963, had dissipated:

Jim and Bob Drew shooting the black-birds that had *colonized* a couple of trees between Lowney's cabin and barracks. Friction with Lowney about how [to do it].***Jim telling a smoker to (G I slang term) strip paper off a butt he (smoker) threw on grass of Colony***Jim's red Jaguar***Lowney's compass on dashboard***days Harry, Al Nash, me poured concrete for new outhouse***electric shuffle board game in Ramada Johnny [Bowers in *The Colony*] mentions***Rex [Bollin] of the 5 gallon hat***me as the "company man," driving Jim's jeep, the

famous jeep he's lugged his trailer around U.S. with.***copies of Village Voice Norman [Mailer] had sent going out with trash***time
Lowney blew up about something: "Who did this?" When no one
answered, she was furious. "Don't tell me you guys are scared of a
woman?"***Lowney saying: "I don't need to drink. I'm already
high."***Harry's scheme to filter water from swimming pool through
hay bails with pump, such as sanitarian workers.

Robb was apparently thinking of writing an essay about the colony, for he
went on:

> Possible opening line:
> Later it [would] always seem a miracle that the Handys—Lowney
> and Harry were home that morning Or was it [had it been] coincidence.
> By "home" I mean that they had driven back from Tucson, Arizona
> to their neat, white house on Mulberry Street in Robinson, Illinois;
> while, at the same time, I, whom they had never met or heard of, was
> hitchhiking west from Philadelphia, my goal rendezvous that same
> house on Mulberry Street, at that time one of the most celebrated (oth-
> ers might say notorious) literary edifices in America. (UIS)

When Robb learned of the existence of the James Jones Literary Society,
founded at Lincoln Trail College in Robinson, Illinois, he wrote a letter,
which was then published in the fall 1993 issue of the *Society Newsletter*:

> When I learned about The James Jones Society from a news item, I was
> gladdened, having spent four summers during the 1950s at the Writer's
> Colony of which Jim was vice president.
> He, and Lowney and Harry Handy, were mammoth influences in
> my life. No one has ever been more generous to me—financially, but
> also regarding their sacrificed time—than were those three.
> I was 19 back in 1953 when I hitchhiked without warning into their
> lives, my appearance no doubt that of the fruitcake Ivy League drop-
> out which I was: Holden Caufield, without a clue. Lowney cited me
> Scripture: "Many are called, but few are chosen." Jones told me, "You're
> tryin' too hard, fella." Harry, sphinx-like, appraised me from above his
> FDR-type cigarette holder. That's how I recall them—almost too big for
> the big screen of memory.
> They also fill my conscience, as perhaps only the dead can, with the
> onerous pressure of an unpaid debt. I idiotically took it for granted they
> would live long enough for me to make restitution for all they'd given.
> Now, a quarter of a century after their departure, I feel more dunned
> than Mr. Micawbar—for I'm in default to ghosts. ("Letter" 4)

Over the years, he came to understand Lowney, Jim, and Harry. As recogni-
tion of their influence, he left half of his estate to the James Jones Literary
Society, to be divided "equally between the general endowment fund for
various Society activities and the First Novel Fellowship."[1] Robb died in 1997.

Robb also wrote "Khaki Moon," which first appeared in the fall 1993 issue of the *Society Newsletter* and was reprinted in *Selected Poems of Charles
Robb*, edited by J. Michael Lennon:

Khaki Moon
for James Jones (1921–1977)

Khaki moon round and large
but a man's steelwool severe voice—
disembodied—calls: "Bull-shit!"
The ghost of James Jones calls:
"Fuck off, son. Moonlight's not khaki.
Tell the truth or shut up."
I try—the moon is round and enormous,
white over the city and to me awful
because James Jones lies dead on Long Island,
they buried Jim Jones in Sagaponack,
nothing fancy—his end—no denouement,
not gunned down at 19 like Prewitt in a golf bunker,
not offed by a Japanese sniper on Guadalcanal
before he could write truths someone had to,
not snipped in his aqua-lung and wet suit
by the grinning Widow-maker,
just sold out by his heart, a very big heart,
leaving a good wife, daughter, and son
and all the work he still hoped to do.

And the moon isn't anything like khaki,
not much is these days,
the Army hasn't worn the color for years,
but Mars is red in the night sky,
moon and city lights too bright to find it
but I guarantee the War-Planet is red
and by its light a million Prewitts are soldiering
for the armies of the world,
ready to kill since their cause is right
or they know who provides a square meal—
and the novels of James Jones can't staunch it
nor all the novels or poems ever written
and the moon is round and big
and asinine as humanity.

But some people one can look up to—
the ghost of James Jones I see doesn't soldier
but in swim trunks vaults on a trampoline
as he jumped in Marshall, Illinois, those summers
at the writers' camp he helped found and maintain,
a short man, muscular and rough-faced

but gentle to all but the pricks,
achieving with pride his somersaults,
half-gainers, back-flips,
the trampoline ringed by strays like me
who dreamed we were writers,
him trying to show it was more than grammar.
Hard to see why a successful writer
gave so much money and time to those
who hadn't made it,
except he knew Mars was still greedy—
the human heart obscene as most (or all)
governments—
one writer all writers helpless against this,
more voices to shout: "No!" the sole chance—
and he taught us how when someone jumps crooked
on a trampoline those on the ground
should break his fall with their hands
and heave him back on the canvas
to continue jumping perhaps,
though where he leaped now we can't help.

(2–3)

Michael Lennon notes in his preface to Robb's poetry, "Charlie's gift has helped transform the Society, enabling it to do even more to encourage interest in the life and works of James Jones, and to encourage the work of unpublished novelists." In the years after Jim left the colony, he continued until the end of his life to help young writers; so, too, did Lowney.

Jon Shirota

The last student in residence at the Handy Colony was Jon Shirota.[2] Jonathan (Jon) Shirota was born in Hawaii to immigrants from Okinawa. After he graduated from high school, he came to the mainland and took a bachelor's degree at Brigham Young University. For several years this aspiring writer worked as an agent in the Internal Revenue Office in Hollywood, "looking forward," as he says, to the day he "could stop bringing miseries into taxpayers' lives" (Shirota narrative). He had worked on a novel *Lucky Come Hawaii*, which was rejected by a New York publisher, and began to correspond with Lowney in 1959. After his first letter, she responded that he should "plan on learning how to make it saleable" (April 11, 1959, UIS). She did not place novels, she said, she taught. Jon should not send her the entire manuscript, she advised, only the first twenty pages and a one-page outline. Lowney assured Jon there would be no charge for her work and that she would make suggestions. She then gave him some boiler-plate advice about concentration, use of flashbacks, etc.—the same sensible advice she had been giving for years (Shirota narrative).

By April 21, she had marked his manuscript "rather severely," but she did not want him to think he was a bad or inferior writer. She thought his sentences were well constructed and that he was groping "toward a good style," and had "much to say."

Although Jim's break from her had been difficult for both of them, she sometimes praised parts of Jim's novels to Jon and other students. She told Jon to look at the way Jim handled transitions in *Eternity* and in *Running* by examining the last page of one chapter and the beginning page of the next chapter. She assured Jon that Jim "put as much time and thought and labor on the transitions as he did the entire chapter."

Jon wanted to come to Marshall, but on May 27, 1959, Lowney explained that Jim no longer supported her work, that Harry was now retired and no longer able to donate four hundred dollars a month; Harry was replaced as superintendent of the refinery in 1954 and was appointed to the newly established position of manager of the Robinson refinery. He held that job for a time before finally retiring. The fifty thousand dollars she had made from the 10 percent of royalties paid by some of the colonists who published had all gone back into the colony. She could not support students in Marshall, but she could help by mail. She advised him to write every day.

Lowney filled her letters with generally helpful advice for Jon, how he could improve his characterizations, his plotting, his narrative drive. She did not often mention her ideas about the occult.

On March 29, 1960, Lowney in a letter praising Jon's improvement told him in a long paragraph that she and Tom Chamales believed in reincarnation and that while he was buried in the Greek Orthodox Church he was really a yogi! "He believed in the eastern theosophical religion," Lowney asserted (Shirota narrative).

Sometimes Lowney praised Jon, other times she heavily marked his manuscripts, saying he was pushing too hard. By November 16, 1961, Lowney's health was poor and she was taking a vacation from teaching. She advised him to send his manuscript to Walter Minton of G. P. Putnam's Sons. Minton rejected the novel, commenting that some of the writing was good but that technical matters had not been mastered. Lowney gave Jon good advice on March 15, 1962: "Don't give up, rewrite, shorten the time covered in the novel, unify the scenes, develop conflict early."

In the letters to Jon after Putnam's had rejected his novel, Lowney was at her best in encouraging him and yet recommending revisions. She suggested he read Uzzell's *The Technique of the Novel*, a practical book that had helped Jim. She also had him write some short stories as a rest from his longer manuscript. Then on March 14, 1963, she wrote Ned Brown, the agent, requesting that Brown consider taking on Jon.

On March 31, 1963, Lowney wrote Jon that Harry had died (of lung cancer), and his novel was then being proofed.[3] Perhaps because he had been persistent, perhaps because she recognized that she would be lonely after Harry's death, she invited Jon to the colony for the summer session. Jon now thinks that Lowney, a Kentuckian, hated revenuers and was testing him all along: "Will I have the guts to quit my job and devote myself full time to finishing *Lucky?*" (Shirota narrative).

The day Jon received the message that she was ready for him to come to the colony, he started packing. The next day he walked into his supervisor's office and resigned. He was up for a promotion then, but he told his boss, who knew nothing about his interest in writing, that he did not ever want to say he had not seized the opportunity.

Jon arrived in Marshall in April 1963 and stayed until late September. He had corresponded with Lowney for four years and felt he knew her quite well. She had come across in letters as a tough, intelligent, no-nonsense woman totally dedicated to writing. "Her letters," he recalls, "also indicated she was a warm, caring person subjected to unpredictable moods."

Early in the cold morning of his arrival, he sat with Lowney in her cabin, in front of her fireplace, and she laid down the law to him. He was to write three hours a day. No more, no less. As he finished each chapter, he was to turn it over to her by sticking the pages under the door to her cabin. She was living in her cabin that spring and summer and would go over his chapters and confer with him. She would prepare meals for him sometimes but generally he was on his own. She left money for food and supplies in the ramada, and the kitchen in that open-aired building was fully operational. Jon could prepare his own meals or go to a local café. Jon did not know that any other students were about until suddenly he heard someone calling:

"Lowney . . . Lowney . . . The damn birds over my roof. They making too much noise. I can't write no more."

Without warning, she grabbed her BB gun. "You goddam white nigger!" she yelled as she rushed to the door. "You get back to your trailer and keep writing or I'll shoot your black ass full of holes!" That was his introduction to the colony: "A mad woman and a writer who couldn't write because the birds over his roof were bothering him." Lowney identified the other colonist there as Charles Wright. Later, Jon dramatizes this scene in *The Last Retreat*.

Jon's turn was next. She asked what Jon was reading, and he mentioned Hemingway. Lowney threw another fit, Jon recalls: "She started throwing Hemingway's books at me. 'You no-good fiddlefucking Chinaman! I don't want any writer of mine ever reading Hemingway. Ever! Any man who blows his head off don't deserve to be read! Gettafuck outa here! You ever read Hemingway again I'm kicking your goddamn Chinaman ass all the way back to California.'" Lowney had forgotten Jon was Japanese. Had she remembered, she would certainly have thrown a fit. She had also forgotten that she had often praised Hemingway for his writing (she had come to object to his cult of masculinity).

About an hour later, Jon remembers, as he was in his barracks cell having serious misgivings about leaving "the safe haven of California and putting my life in the hands of a crazy woman, there was a knock on my cabin door. There she was. The crazy woman. Was I in for more of her 'Chinaman' treatment?" Lowney, though, was now an entirely different person. He noticed she had been crying:

> She apologized, almost sobbingly, for what took place in her cabin earlier. She then told me what she had been going through ever since her husband, Harry, died [a few months previously]. She and Harry had been married for many years. She had not realized how much she had depended on him. Now, she missed him. Terribly. She felt abandoned. Left alone. Cast aside. No one and nobody to talk to, to look forward and share with, to understand her like Harry had all those years.
>
> And there was Harry's unfinished novel. Will she be able to finish it for him. Make Harry's dream come true? Of having a novel of his own published?
>
> I could say nothing. She was my teacher; I her pupil. Not only as a student of writing, but of fathoming my very existence. I had put my life in her hands, depended on her, trusted her all these years. And now this. She was reaching out. For my help! For my understanding! For my sympathy!
>
> I found myself reaching over and touching her hand, head low, tears streaming down my face. No words. Just sharing her agony. Hating myself for feeling sorry for myself. (Shirota narrative)

It was not, Jon knows, an auspicious start, but he can now say: "as the days went on [it was] very rewarding, very enlightening. A rebirth. A catharsis. A cleansing of the soul."

Lowney explained during that first conversation that the other colony resident for the 1963 session was Charles (Charlie) Wright, whose novel the *Messenger* had been accepted by Farrar, Straus, and Giroux. Lowney said that Charlie was living in one of the trailers on the grounds, and Jon was to go into a barracks room. She urged Jon not to get too cozy with Charlie for, as Jon reconstructs her views, "she was afraid I would go on a binge with him, raise hell, and not do any writing." When Wright visited him the first night Jon was there, Jon made himself clear: He was only interested in finishing *Lucky Come Hawaii*. Nothing else.

In the days that followed, Jon wrote three hours a day, and Jon and Charlie would get together for brief moments when they were preparing and eating meals in the ramada. Lowney had relaxed her views on drinking. She supplied Charlie with bottles of vermouth, and he was drunk most of the time. Jon felt sorry for Charlie, who was in a small lily-white town. There was no social life for him there. The only other black in Marshall was Squab Wilson.

About two weeks after Jon arrived, Charlie suddenly left. Lowney had taken Jon out for a ride early one evening, showing him various places he could eat. Sitting in front of the bus station was Charlie and his bag. Lowney commented: "I knew he wouldn't be sticking around any longer. His book is coming out and he's got ants in his pants." Jon says that Lowney was not angry with Charlie for leaving without saying goodbye. She was pleased that his book would soon be published. Every manuscript she vetted was another sign that her method worked.

Jon would turn in a chapter, and Lowney would mark it up with her usual scrawls in the margin. He would go through the chapter again. Lowney would mark it again. Jon says as the days went by the writing and rewriting and his becoming used to the isolation and quiet of the Marshall compound began to work. His writing became better. Although she was critical of his words on the page, Lowney kept encouraging him.

After Jon had written for ten days or so, Lowney would tell him to get out of Marshall. "Go get drunk; go get laid. Just don't do it in Marshall," she would tell him. He had some Hawaiian friends in Chicago, and off he would head for Chicago and go on a rampage. Driving back to Marshall, usually with a hangover, he would prepare himself again for the isolated life and feel happy to be back writing.

What did Jon do when he was not writing? His cabin was next to the swimming pool, which was then in disrepair. He would lie on the diving board and watch the rabbits and squirrels in the grass and bushes. He also mowed the lawn. That was another of Lowney's laws. He was to keep all the acres trimmed. After a light lunch, he would fill the lawn mower with gas and keep mowing until the gas ran out. He would repeat it the next day, and it usually took him four days to complete the task.

At times Lowney would cook for him. Sometimes she would gather mushrooms on the grounds and prepare them in her special way. They would then sit on the steps of her cabin and talk for hours, first about his novel, then about her family, her brothers and sisters, her father who had been a sheriff. Jon was an admirer of Jones's novels, but Lowney would curse him (she knew original curses Jon had never even heard before) if he dwelled too much on Jim Jones. He had to be careful and say little about *From Here to Eternity* and *Some Came Running*. She was grief stricken that spring and summer, and Jon now says, "Because I was so involved selfishly, in my novel, I didn't fully appreciate what she was going through about Harry's death."

In Jon's view one of Lowney's extraordinary characteristics was that, although she was from a southern family, she was "color blind." From his conversations with her, Jon realized she did not give a damn what race or nationality anyone was. She was interested in human beings. "As for me being a Japanese," Jon says, "she didn't give a damn." Before he knew her, he thought she would. "After all," he says, "'We' were the enemy in Jim's *Eter-*

nity. One day, a lady from Robinson comes to visit Lowney. The lady finds out I'm a 'Jap.' She immediately wants to loan Lowney a gun to protect herself." Lowney and Jon laughed at the narrow-minded attitude.

Jon worked hard that summer. Lowney kept giving him advice, for she believed in his promise as a writer and arranged to have Ned Brown become his agent. At the end of the session in late September, Jon left, expecting to come back to the colony in following years, but Lowney died the following June. The colony never reopened.

After that summer of 1963, Lowney went to Arizona first, then back to Florida. Harry's death brought changes into her life just as the break with Jim had done. Her letters to Jon indicate she was more in control than she had been in times of crisis with Jim and that she remained her spunky self. She argued that some editors could not recognize good work and congratulated him when Bantam accepted his novel.

In Florida she bought a house and once more became a part of Don's life. Lowney and Don would go out for meals and have good conversations, but she was back again trying to control Don's life. She wanted him to buy the house next to the one she had purchased. Now mature and financially successful, he found he could just about keep Lowney from running his life yet stay on good terms with her. She had been hit hard by Harry's death for she had not realized how much she depended on him until he was gone. He was the brick wall she had leaned on. She said to Don, "People saw me as the do-er with energy to burn, but it was from Harry that I drew my strength" (Sackrider narrative).

Those months after Harry's death she did recover much of her strength, though. She resumed helping pregnant girls, again she came into Willard Lindsay's life and assisted him. Don found her the same brilliant conversationalist she had always been. Scrappy Lowney was, as she had always been, even in the last year of her life. She wrote Jon on January 20, 1964, that she was going to open a publishing house: "And if Bantam Books fails to find you a hardback publisher—THIS IS WHAT THEY DID TO JERE PEACOCK—had nine houses turn him down so they could save money and hog it all—BUT I WILL PUBLISH YOU AND JERE BOTH. I can get plenty of money; you'd be surprised at the backing and where I am getting it" (Shirota narrative). The publishing venture did not materialize.

Who could have qualms about Jon's feeling of love and admiration for Lowney? She worked with him when he was rejected by a publisher, she encouraged him, she fought for him with editors and agents, she offered to publish him in hardback if no one else would.

Jon's novel *Lucky Come Hawaii* is set in Hawaii at the time of Pearl Harbor. It was fitting that the novel to come from the last colonist in residence on the Marshall grounds dealt with much the same time period as *Eternity*, the first novel from the colony, but Jon offered some quite different perspectives from Jim's. The father in the fictional family, an Okinawa-born farmer, expected the Japanese forces to capture the Hawaiian Islands, but his children, Americanized, saw the world differently than their father did. The conflict in the novel is psychologically sound, and Jon had a light, sometimes comic touch to his handling of the material. *Lucky Come Hawaii* is still in print. In the *Honolulu Star Bulletin* for January 7, 1966, Saburo Kido wrote of this novel, which deserves even wider attention: "As far as I am concerned, *Lucky Come Hawaii* is the most exciting and mature novel written and published by a fellow Japanese-American" (3).

Jon came to realize, as did Don Sackrider and other colonists who had known her well, that despite Lowney's outward coarseness and toughness, "she was very tender, caring, and vulnerable. Words like fiddlefucking motherfucker, cunt, asshole, etc., would stream out of her mouth one moment, then her eyes would be filled with tears the next when she talked about the handicapped and the social ills in the world" (Shirota narrative). Almost all the colonists also learned how to interpret her tirades, how to get out of her way when she was in her dark moods, for she tended to forget and forgive.

Jon, in a remarkable eulogy, says that Lowney gave him life, wisdom, and hope. She gave him a reprieve from death. From self-destruction: "She gave me a reason to live; not merely exist. I learned more about myself from her than I learned from my own mother. And my mother was a warm, kind, and wise mother. Lowney taught not only writing; she taught life. She made me aware why I did all the crazy things I did as a young man; why I was still doing all those crazy things. She never judged. Her answer was always, 'People like you had to go through all that.'" Lowney made him feel for others and realize that his life had not been a waste but one with much promise yet to be fulfilled. He sees her as a teacher of human behavior: "She was brutally honest. At times unbearably so." She was, though, a person who brought about changes in the lives of those she taught: "She was consummately selfless," he believes. "Totally dedicated." He believed in her completely, and she helped make him a better person and a better writer. "Lowney was a great lady, someone who deserves far more than she has been credited [with] in the past."

Epilogue

In Lowney's last letter to Jon Shirota in the late spring of 1964, before she died in her sleep on June 27, she said she had never seen the Handy Colony as beautiful as it was that year. Her house, the barracks, the ramada, the swimming pool, the trailers, the brick walkways were all still in place, but no students came that summer or ever again. The grounds are still there. Lowney's house is gone; only the chimney stands. Harry's cabin is gone, and his faithful support of Lowney and his work in overseeing the building of the Handy Colony and making major financial contributions to it over the years is almost forgotten. The barracks are moved. The trailers are gone. The swimming pool is gone but the gently sloping banks remain, covered with grass. The ramada still stands. The brick walkways are gone. In spring, summer, fall, and winter, the former cow pasture that was once the Handy Colony is beautiful and peaceful. Just at the entrance of the colony grounds stands Jim's striking bachelor house, just as it was when he lived there, just as it was the day Lowney ran him off with his wife.[1] This house and the Handy Colony grounds are a reminder of an experimental writing colony that existed both informally and formally from 1943 to 1963.

Lowney believed she could teach anyone to write, and she brought to the colony a few deadbeats, but many of her students were indeed talented. She did take chances. She was not afraid to give renegades, castaways, blacks, and Japanese Americans a chance. Copying was not a panacea for beginning writers, but there was a certain logic in the method. She did try to get students to write every day; and over and over she stressed discipline. She read and reread manuscripts and generally gave good advice. She demanded revisions. She knew how to make students feel they had her complete attention and that they were making progress, that they were going to succeed. She believed in them completely and willed their successes. She also taught self-examination and thus the power of self-knowledge to heal—no mean feat when dealing with people in pain. These were her most admirable qualities.

Lowney was often given to emotional outbursts. Some of her actions seem irrational, and she tried to micromanage the lives of her students. She forbade them to talk about their work to other colonists, even though such conversation would undoubtedly have been intellectually stimulating. She did not stress theoretical material enough and sometimes posed as an anti-intellectual. Some professors in established masters of fine arts in creative writing courses have been and are as quirky as she, and she was as successful with her students as many creative writing teachers have been. Her success, however, was as a teacher, not as a writer.

Lowney did help Jim Jones become a major American writer. He wrote some of his best work (*From Here to Eternity* and *Some Came Running*) during the fourteen years they were together. She believed in him from the first day they met. She and Harry supported him while he learned the art and craft of writing. And Jim learned much from her, but after his departure from Marshall he spoke little—and then warily—about Harry and Lowney, her influence on him, and the Handy Colony itself. He learned discipline from her. He wrote daily.

After his marriage to Gloria, he wrote some of his best work (*The Pistol, The Thin Red Line, Whistle*). It is true that he was happier with Gloria than he had been with Lowney; Gloria was fun-loving and also a good critic. The Joneses and their two children lived a life in Europe far different from the one he had shared with Lowney, but that life belongs to a different story. Jim transferred his affections from Lowney to Gloria and the children (something Lowney warned him against), but the literary lessons he learned from Lowney stayed with him, and with age he became a better, deeper writer than he was when he left Illinois. He died on May 9, 1977, as he neared the end of writing *Whistle*, the last volume of his war trilogy.

Many other writers at the Handy Colony finally published: John Bowers, Tom T. Chamales, Edwin C. (Sonny) Daly, William Duhart, David Ray, Robert Kendall, Willard Lindsay, Jere Peacock, Jon Shirota, Gerald Tesch (Jerry Tschappat), and Charles Wright. Others profited from studying, even informally, with Lowney, for she made them better readers, writers, and thinkers: Tinks Howe, Mary Ann Jones, Charles Robb, and Don Sackrider, to name just a few. Lowney believed in them and provided for all of them a philosophic approach to life to be accepted or rejected. Most of her students felt that Lowney had profoundly affected their lives and their artistic aspirations.

Epilogue

What happened to Lowney's students? The outline of James Jones's life and work is known, and he is clearly one of the best of American war novelists. Tom Chamales, after completing two novels, was killed in a fire, his career cut short. Mary Ann Jones died before she completed her promising novel. Bowers reported to Wood and Keating that "dippy Tschappat . . . died from a busted marriage, busted hope, and too many stimulants" (Preface xi). Tinks Howe married Helen Whitlock, who became a professor of English at Lincoln Trail College in Robinson and was instrumental in founding the James Jones Literary Society; Tinks worked at the refinery there until his retirement. Jon Shirota became a successful writer and playwright. Don Sackrider became a commercial airline pilot and, after retiring, is much involved in the activities of the James Jones Literary Society, as are Helen and Tinks. John Bowers is a writer and editor in New York. David Ray has had a long and distinguished career as a writer and editor. Charles Wright continues to publish. Willard Lindsay may yet write his account of Lowney and the Handy Colony. Of the others, some published, some did not, and some just faded away.

Lowney, as editor, urged her students to write commercial books but not to pander to the tastes of any segments of the reading public. She listened and followed several different drummers and believed in many of the transcendental ideas of Emerson, Thoreau, and Whitman and the theosophical beliefs of Madame Blavatsky and Annie Besant. She was a New Ager. She was a radical, just as Cash Clay had been. The colony founded by Lowney, Harry, and Jim had its successes and failures. It was unique. The experimental Handy Colony, its founders, and its students, all deserve to be remembered for their contributions to American literature.

Notes

Bibliography

Index

Notes

Introduction: Lowney, Harry, Jim, and the Colony

1. One exception was the popular mystery novelist Frances Crane, a personal friend of both Lowney and Harry from nearby Lawrenceville, Illinois, who encouraged Lowney to write and to help Jones with his novel. Maxwell Aley in New York had once been Crane's agent, and for a time Aley represented Jones as well. Lowney recalled that she had met one editor in New York before she met Jones, but that editor was not interested in her novel.

1. Lowney Turner Handy: The Early Life of a "Literary Angel"

1. For information about Lowney Turner Handy's early life, we are especially indebted to her sister's memoirs: Vivian Turner McClellan, *One in the Middle*.

2. James Jones in his second published novel, *Some Came Running*, has the character Gwen French allowing people to believe she was promiscuous, although she was in fact a virgin. Lowney gave no indication that she recognized herself in the fictional portrayal of Gwen French.

2. James Jones: The Early Years of a Returning Soldier Who "Wants to Write"

1. For information about the Jones family and about James Jones, we are especially indebted to Frank MacShane, *Into Eternity: The Life of James Jones*, and to George Hendrick, ed., *To Reach Eternity: The Letters of James Jones*.

2. It is useful to remember the distinction between army regulars, who enlisted in peacetime before World War II, and draftees, who were conscripted during the war. In *From Here to Eternity*, Jones wrote specifically about the regular army.

3. Several members of the James Jones Literary Society were in Hawaii in the spring of 1995, and they dedicated a plaque at Makapuu Point. The plaque reads: "In November, 1941, James Jones, author of the classic Army novel, *From Here to Eternity* (1951), and his company (Company F, 27th Regiment, 25th Division) built five pillboxes on the ridge in front of you. On December 7, 1941, Jones and his fellow soldiers occupied the pillboxes with machine guns and rifles to stop potential enemy forces from marching to Honolulu. The Makapuu Head pillboxes were immortalized in *The Pistol* (1959), one of Jones' other novels."

3. The Beginnings of *From Here to Eternity* and of the Handy Colony

1. Also of interest in any study of Jones and Emersonianism is Greg Randle, "James Jones's First Romance: An Examination of 'They Shall Inherit the Laughter'" (unpublished master's thesis, Sangamon State University, 1989), in the Handy Colony Collection, University of Illinois at Springfield.

2. Five years after divorcing Don's father, Don's mother married Tom Wrenn in 1943. Don, his brother, and the newlyweds lived together in a modest house in Robinson. Later, his grandmother Miller came to live with them.

5. The Colony Gets Under Way in Marshall, Illinois

1. In "Two Legs for the Two of Us," Jones based the story of a veteran who had lost a leg in the war on a friend of his. His friend in real life was having a hard time adjusting to civilian life, and Lowney, Jim, and Mary Ann agreed to lift his spirits and his ego by having Mary Ann sleep with him. Jim and Lowney were clearly not concerned enough, in this instance, about Mary Ann's troubled state. MacShane writes of Mary Ann's death that "she had a seizure, caused by a brain tumor, during which she swallowed her tongue." He continues that Jim and his brother, Jeff, had known about her tumor and taken her for medical treatments that were supposed to have cured it" (127–28). Their uncle Charlie had her death investigated, but the jury found that she had indeed died of natural causes. Jim again cut his ties with his uncle.

6. Real Life and Fiction at the Colony

1. Don has a different view of Ted:

> When Russ Meskimen appeared at Lowney's table and was introduced as someone from Hollywood I was at first surprised that Ted had a brother and that he was so totally different from Ted. I knew Ted only as the owner of the furniture store where my maternal Grandmother Miller frequently bought furniture. When I lived with Grandmother Miller I frequently was sent to make the one- and two-dollar payment on her account. Sometimes I saw Ted and he was always friendly to me. Years later my mother told me much more about Ted: how he tried to date her, said she was the only decent girl in town. Once when she was on her way home from the ice cream shop where she worked after school while she was in high school, Ted was driving by when a man was annoying her. Ted stopped and beat the man up. Mother said that her mother had encouraged her to go with Ted. Ted flattered Grandmother Miller because she was Polly's

mother, and later whenever my grandmother was late in payments on the furniture, Ted never made anything of it. (Sackrider narrative)

2. Don believes the Robinson rumor mill may well have been working overtime:

> My Grandmother Sackrider worked for the Meskimens as a cleaning lady. Jim combined my two grandmothers as Jane in the novel, never bothering to change my Grandmother Miller's name. Jim did not keep them in character. Neither one would have appeared downtown without being very well dressed with straight seams in their stockings and a hat. Neither would have stopped for a beer on the way home from work as Jane did in *Some Came Running*. Grandmother Sackrider was treated as one of the family by Emily Meskimen, Ted's wife. Going to work there was more of a social occasion than work. Emily and my mother had been close friends around the time I was born. After my parents were divorced I don't remember seeing Emily at our house. My mother could never see Ted Meskimen as a boyfriend or husband. I think she and I thought of him as a Jack Benny character. (Sackrider narrative)

Helen Howe agrees that Ted was "cheap and stingy" but feels he lacked the gentleness and class of Benny. Tinks disliked Ted and found it difficult to be civil to him (Howe narrative).

Jones's characterization of Jane was obviously drawn from several people in Robinson in addition to Don's grandmothers. Helen believes Jones made major use of a jovial bleached blonde divorcee who was often in the local pubs and often left with a man. Ted's wife, Helen says, would never have allowed this woman in her house, but she was known to Jim and all his friends as a larger-than-life character. She cleaned house for Arkie and Russ when they lived together.

7. Colonists Get Published and Jim Leaves for New York

1. When Jerry first appeared at the colony, the early colonists all chuckled at how much Tschappat reminded them of the younger Jim Jones, not only in appearance but in his cockiness. Jim's sister, Mary Ann, was the first to notice, and then they all did, including Lowney. Jim was not amused (Sackrider narrative).

8. Jim's Marriage and Its Consequences for the Colony

1. Don believes that Lowney had made the choice to see Jim become "a great writer," and it had become a trap from which she could not easily escape. At certain times she wanted to be free of her Jamie, but she loved him and cared for him and could not see how to get out of the trap of her own making (Sackrider narrative).

2. Don went to see Jim in 1968 in Paris. The two had not seen each other since the fall of 1956, not long before Jim and Gloria met and were married. Jim told Don that Gloria wanted nothing to do with anyone from Illinois. Don did meet her and told her he wanted to her friend." He also told her he had loved Lowney and did not want to hear anything bad about her. They were to leave Lowney out of all their conversations, just as Jim and Gloria had decided to do. This worked for Gloria and Don, just as it had worked for Gloria and Jim. They were all on friendly terms. Later Jim

and Don adjourned to a neighborhood bar. Don told Jim he thought his treatment of Lowney in *Go to the Widow-Maker* was unfair, that it was not a true picture. Jim agreed, at least partially, by saying his portrait of her in *Widow-Maker* was incomplete, that she should also have been shown as she was when she was younger. Jim also said that Lowney "had gone off the deep end with Eastern religions." Don told Jim he knew Jim had to be on his own, away from Lowney. Jim agreed, saying, "Yes, she tried to take over your life in Miami" (Sackrider narrative).

9. The Final Years

1. The James Jones Literary Society gives a yearly award to a writer at work on a first novel.

2. During the summer of 1963 Lowney also helped Robert Kendall, Tom Chamales's cousin, by correspondence. Kendall's nonfiction *White Teacher in a Black School* was published in 1964 by Devin-Adair. Kendall had been an actor in Hollywood and a ministerial student before he became a teacher in a black school. He had few sympathies with his students—and even fewer for the administrators of the school system. Kendall's is the only nonfiction book that Lowney encouraged and vetted. She undoubtedly worked with Kendall because of her admiration for Chamales and for his fiction.

3. Harry's novel, *Turnaround*, was completed by Lowney after his death but was never published. The title refers to the annual repair of a unit within a refinery. Only chapter 4 survives in the Handy Collection. The chapter is competently written and shows Harry was writing about what he knew best—the business and social life in a Midwestern town. The entire manuscript was located in October 2000.

Epilogue

1. The house that Jones built in Marshall is privately owned and thus is not open to the public.

Bibliography

Published Writings by Students of Lowney Handy Composed During Their Colony Years

Chamales, Tom T. *Go Naked in the World*. New York: Scribner's, 1959.

———. *Never So Few*. New York: Scribner's, 1957.

Daly, Edwin C. *Some Must Watch*. New York: Scribner's, 1957. Daly, who lived in Marshall, was a day student at the colony.

Duhart, William C. *The Deadly Pay-Off*. Greenwich: Gold Medal, 1958.

Jones, James. *From Here to Eternity*. New York: Scribner's, 1951. Rpt., New York: Avon, 1975. (Page citations are to the reprint edition.)

———. *The Ice-Cream Headache and Other Stories*. New York: Delacorte, 1968. Stories from Jones's colony period include "The Temper of Steel," "Just Like the Girl," "The Way It Is," "Two Legs for the Two of Us," "Secondhand Man," "None Sing So Wildly," "Greater Love," "The King," and "The Valentine." The last four stories—"A Bottle of Cream," "Sunday Allergy," "The Tennis Game," and "The Ice-Cream Headache"—were written in 1957 after his break with Lowney.

———. *Some Came Running*. New York: Scribner's, 1958.

Kendall, Robert. *White Teacher in a Black School*. New York: Devin-Adair, 1964. Kendall was a correspondence student.

Lindsay, Willard. "A Busy Day." *Ladies Home Journal*, September 1949. Lindsay was a day student but often traveled with Lowney and Jim.

Peacock, Jere. *To Drill and Die*. New York: Bantam Books, 1964.

———. *Valhalla*. New York: Putnam's, 1961.

Pevehouse, Alvin. "The Kachina Dolls." *Ellery Queen's Mystery Magazine*, May 1957, 41–55. Pevehouse, a minister with a church in Marshall, was a day student.

Shirota, Jon. *Lucky Come Hawaii*. New York: Bantam Books, 1965.

Tesch, Gerald, pseud. [Jerry Tschappat]. *Never the Same Again*. New York: Putnam's, 1956.

Wright, Charles. *The Messenger*. New York: Farrar, 1963.

Other Works

Adelman, George. "Never the Same Again." *Library Journal* 15 Nov. 1956: 2693.

"The Art of Fiction XXIII: James Jones." *Paris Review* 20 (1959): 35–55.

Baro, Gene. Rev. of *Go Naked in the World*, by Tom T. Chamales. *New York Herald Tribune*, 31 Jan. 1960: 6.

Bowers, John. *The Colony*. New York: Dutton, 1971.

———. Preface. *James Jones in Illinois: A Guide to the Handy Writers' Colony Collection in the Sangamon State University Archives*. By Thomas J. Wood and Meredith Keating. Springfield, Ill.: Sangamon State University, 1989.

Cantwell, Robert E. "James Jones: Another 'Eternity'?" *Newsweek* 23 Nov. 1953: 102+.

Carter, Steven R. *James Jones: An American Literary Orientalist Master*. Urbana: U of Illinois P, 1998.

Dempsey, David. "Marines at Ease." *New York Times Book Review* 8 Jan. 1961: 3.

———. "Tough and Tormented, This Was the Army to Mr. Jones." *New York Times Book Review* 25 Feb. 1951: 2.

Garrett, George. *James Jones*. San Diego: Harcourt, 1984.

Gehman, Richard. "Blockbuster Lands: Greeted with a Yawn." *Chicago Tribune Magazine of Books* 15 Jan. 1961: 3.

Geismar, Maxwell. Rev. of *Never So Few*, by Tom T. Chamales. *Saturday Review* 23 Mar. 1957: 12–13.

Giles, James R. *James Jones*. Boston: Twayne, 1981.

"The Good Life of James Jones." *Life* 11 Feb. 1957: 83+.

Hicks, Granville. "James Jones's 'Some Came Running': A Study in Arrogant Primitivism." *New Leader* 27 Jan. 1958: 20–22.

Hoey, R. A. Rev. of *Never So Few*, by Tom T. Chamales. *Library Journal* 15 Mar. 1957: 12–13.

"Housemother Knows Best." *Time* 12 Nov. 1956: 128.

Howe, Helen, and Tinks Howe. Unpublished narrative, in the possession of the authors.

Jones, James. *Go to the Widow-Maker*. New York: Delacorte, 1967.

———. "James Jones." *Twentieth Century Authors*, 1st supp. Ed. Stanley Kunitz, 500–501. New York: Wilson, 1955.

———. *The James Jones Reader*. Ed. James R. Giles and J. Michael Lennon. New York: Carol, 1991.

———. *The Pistol*. New York: Scribner's, 1959.

———. *The Thin Red Line*. New York: Scribner's, 1963.

———. *To Reach Eternity: The Letters of James Jones*. Ed. George Hendrick. New York: Random, 1989.

———. *WW II: A Chronicle of Soldiering*. New York: Grosset, 1975.

Kash, Steve. "Colonial History: Marshall's Handy Colony for Writers Left a Mark on American Literature." *Terre Haute Tribune Star* 14 June 1998: B1+.

Kido, Saburo. Rev. of *Lucky Come Hawaii*, by Jon Shirota. *Honolulu Star Bulletin* 7 Jan. 1966: 3.

Bibliography

La Farge, Oliver. Rev. of *Some Must Watch*, by Edwin C. Daly. *Saturday Review* 23 Mar. 1957: 12–13.

Lennon, J. Michael. "Glimpses: James Jones 1921–1977." *Paris Review* 103 (summer 1987): 205–36. Transcripts from the PBS documentary *James Jones: Reveille to Taps*, produced by J. Michael Lennon and Jeffrey Van Davis.

Leonard, William. "She Teaches Tough Guys to Write." *Chicago Sunday Tribune Magazine* 14 July 1957: 18–19.

MacShane, Frank. *Into Eternity: The Life of James Jones*. Boston: Houghton, 1985.

McClellan, Vivian Turner. *One in the Middle*. Galatia, Ill.: B & W, 1987.

Morris, Willie. *James Jones: A Friendship*. Garden City: Doubleday, 1978.

Randle, Greg. "James Jones's First Romance: An Examination of 'They Shall Inherit the Laughter.'" Unpublished master's thesis, 1989. Handy Colony Collection, University of Illinois at Springfield.

Ray, David. "Mrs. Handy's Curious Colony." *Chicago Magazine* September 1956: 22–27.

———. "Mrs. Handy's Recipes for Writers." *New Republic* 22 April 1957: 19–20.

Rev. of *Never So Few*, by Tom T. Chamales. *Kirkus* 15 Jan. 1957: 45.

Richardson, H. Edward. *Cassius Marcellus Clay: Firebrand of Freedom*. Lexington: UP of Kentucky, 1976.

Robb, Charles. "Letter to the Society." *James Jones Society* Fall 1993: 4.

———. *Selected Poems of Charles Robb*. Ed. with a preface by J. Michael Lennon. Robinson, Ill.: James Jones Literary Soc., 1998.

Sackrider, Don. Unpublished narrative, including letters of Lowney Handy to Sackrider, in the possession of the author.

Shirota, Jon. *The Last Retreat*. Unpublished play.

———. Unpublished narrative, including letters of Lowney Handy to Shirota, in the possession of the author.

UIS. Archives of the University of Illinois at Springfield. For details of the Handy collection, see Thomas J. Wood and Meredith Keating, *James Jones in Illinois: A Guide to the Handy Writers' Colony Collection*.

Uzzell, Thomas. *The Technique of the Novel: A Handbook on the Craft of the Long Narrative*. New York: Citadel, 1959.

Whipple, A. B. C. "James Jones and His Angel: His Talent Lay Buried Under Frustration and Rebellion Until an Illinois Housewife Made Him Write 'From Here to Eternity.'" *Life* 7 May 1951: 142+.

Wood, Thomas J. "'Not Following in the Groove': Lowney Handy, James Jones, and the Handy Colony for Writers." *Illinois Historical Journal* 90 (summer 1997): 82–96.

Wood, Thomas J., and Meredith Keating. *James Jones in Illinois: A Guide to the Handy Writers' Colony Collection in the Sangamon State University Archives*. Springfield, Ill.: Sangamon State University, 1989.

"Writer's Colony." *Sepia* Dec. 1957: 36–40.

"Writers' Colony: Woman Who Trained James Jones Is Tutoring Two Negro Authors." *Ebony* Nov. 1957: 114+.

Index

GEORGE HENDRICK, who served as first president of the James Jones Literary Society, edited *To Reach Eternity: The Letters of James Jones*. He lives in Urbana, Illinois.

HELEN HOWE is a retired professor of English at Lincoln Trail College in Robinson, where she taught American literature, composition, and creative writing. Her husband, Tinks, was a friend of James Jones since childhood. The Howes were close personal friends of Lowney and Harry Handy and live in Robinson.

DON SACKRIDER, a retired airline captain, was born in Robinson. Only the second student to join the Handy Colony, he remained associated with it through 1953. He lives in Key Biscayne, Florida, and Whidby Island, Washington.